WOOD-FIRED OVEN
COOKBOOK

WOOD-FIRED OVEN
COOKBOOK

70 recipes for incredible stone-baked pizzas and breads, roasts, cakes and desserts, all specially devised for the outdoor oven and illustrated in over 400 photographs

HOLLY AND DAVID JONES
PHOTOGRAPHY BY JAKE EASTHAM

This edition is published by Aquamarine
an imprint of Anness Publishing Ltd
info@anness.com

www.aquamarinebooks.com
www.annesspublishing.com

If you like the images in this book and would
like to investigate using them for publishing,
promotions or advertising, please visit our
website www.practicalpictures.com
for more information.

© Anness Publishing Ltd 2022

Publisher: Joanna Lorenz
Editorial Director: Helen Sudell
Executive Editor: Joanne Rippin
Designer: Nigel Partridge
Photographer: Jake Eastham
Food Stylist: Fergal Connolly
Props Stylist: Julia Meadowcroft
Production Controller: Ben Worley

With thanks to the following for kind
permission to photograph their ovens: Andy
Platt, Slapton Ley Field Centre; James Dart;
and Marc Millon. Thanks also to Amrit Row,
www.woodfiredoven.co.uk for supplying tools
and equipment.

A CIP catalogue record for this book is
available from the British Library.

PUBLISHER'S NOTE
Although the advice and information in this
book are believed to be accurate and true at
the time of going to press, neither the authors
nor the publisher can accept any legal
responsibility or liability for any errors or
omissions that may have been made nor for
any inaccuracies nor for any loss, harm or
injury that comes about from following
instructions or advice in this book.

NOTES
• Bracketed terms are intended for
American readers.
• For all recipes, quantities are given in both
metric and imperial measures and, where
appropriate, in standard cups and spoons.
Follow one set of measures, but not a mixture,
because they are not interchangeable.
• Standard spoon and cup measures are level.
1 tsp = 5ml, 1 tbsp = 15ml, 1 cup = 250ml/8fl oz.
• Australian standard tablespoons are 20ml.
Australian readers should use 3 tsp in place of
1 tbsp for measuring small quantities.
• American pints are 16fl oz/2 cups. American
readers should use 20fl oz/2.5 cups in place of
1 pint when measuring liquids.
• The nutritional analysis given for each recipe
is calculated per portion (i.e. serving or item),
unless otherwise stated. If the recipe gives a
range, such as Serves 4–6, then the nutritional
analysis will be for the smaller portion size,
i.e. 6 servings. The analysis does not include
optional ingredients.
• Medium (US large) eggs are used unless
otherwise stated.

CONTENTS

INTRODUCTION

The rise in popularity of the wood-fired oven is just part of a centuries-long tradition. Very similar in design to the first ovens used in the ancient world, the ovens now available in kit form are direct descendants from the pot ovens of Egypt, the brick ovens of Classical Greece and Rome, and the communal village ovens of medieval Europe.

Humans have been using fire to cook food for thousands of years, and ovens have been dated to 29,000BC. The very first ovens were fire pits in which food would be cooked in the flames, or wrapped in leaves, an early method still used today in Asia, where food is protected by banana leaves in charcoal braziers. Fire pits are still used for cooking (often for tourists) in Hawaii, New Zealand and Africa.

Initially food was cooked in the fire itself or in a pot in the fire. From there, humans developed the skills of baking by putting a lidded pot in the fire and covering it with embers to create an oven where the food was cooked inside.

EGYPTIAN CLAY POTS

The ancient Egyptians document a variety of domestic ovens, from covered pots in the fire's embers to purpose-built brick ovens in which the dough was stuck to the inside walls until cooked – a definite precursor to the tandoor we know today.

GREEK BREAD OVENS

The ovens of ancient Greece were the first front-loaded ovens, and it was the Greeks who developed baking into a profession.

▼ *Some of the earliest surviving ovens can be seen in the ruins of Pompeii, Italy.*

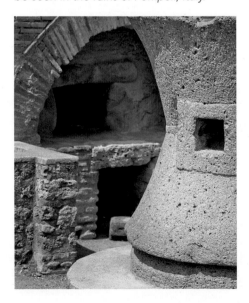

▲ *These Egyptian bread ovens take their shape from the original pots used to bake bread in ancient times.*

They also developed a range of bread and bakery products. In the home a small domed oven would sit over the fire on a tripod with the fire heating it from below.

ROMAN OVENS

The wood-fired ovens we use today are close in design to the ones found in the Roman excavations in Pompeii, showing how little they have changed. The ovens in Pompeii are in various stages of disrepair – for some, just the chimney remains, while for others, the whole oven is intact, revealing seasoned terracotta bricks and tiles. Like the ancient Greeks, the Romans had professional bakeries in each district as well, as having an oven in their own homes.

INDIAN TANDOOR

The tandoor oven has been used for generations throughout the Middle East and Asia. The fire sits in the bottom of the cylindrical oven so the heat rises upward, cooking anything in the way – breads slapped on to the oven's sides or spicy marinated meat on metal racks in its centre. The tandoor has now travelled around the world with the local Indian restaurant and is sometimes fired with gas or electricity rather than the traditional charcoal or wood. The tandoor oven produces food that is chargrilled and crispy on the outside but still moist and tender on the inside.

EUROPEAN COMMUNAL OVENS

The communal bread oven was pivotal to village life in Europe for many centuries. Once the baker had made the daily village bread, the village women would bring their evening meals to bake in the residual heat of the oven, no doubt catching up on the daily goings-on and the latest gossip in the process.

On the Greek islands as recently as the 1980s, the village women would still take their evening meals to the bakers at 11am, after he had finished the day's baking. They would then pay a few drachmas for him to put their meals in the oven to use the residual heat for slow-cooking their dishes all afternoon. Prunings from the olive trees would be stored and used as kindling along with those from the almond trees. When the fire was lit, the base of the oven would be brushed out with a bundle of fresh rosemary branches to act as a disinfectant, also giving off the most wonderful fragrance in the heat. The ashes from the fire would be used as a fertilizer, and renewing the black colour of the

▲ *The traditional Russian oven was the heart of the home and was even slept on during the bitter winter months.*

▲ *Some of the communal ovens in Greece are still used by villagers for baking bread and for the Sunday meal.*

village women's clothes, in the whitewash for the houses and to help keep insects at bay. Nothing would be wasted.

Today in Transylvania the wood-fired oven is still used on a regular basis. In many villages each house has its own wood-fired oven in the yard, which is fired up every few days to bake for the household. Even in the winters, which are extremely cold, the bread is made in these outside wood-fired ovens. First to go in the oven are the breads, and then the falling temperatures are used to bake meat dishes, vegetable dishes and cakes.

In other countries with extreme winters, such as Russia, villagers would lie on top of the wood-fired oven so they would have a warm, cosy bed. So important was the communal oven in Russian life that it assumed life-giving properties in Russian story-telling, when invalids who hadn't walked for years would leap to their feet after a night spent on the warmth of the top of the village oven.

PIZZA OVENS AND THE REVIVAL

Any holiday to Italy would be incomplete without a trip to a pizzeria, where you'll enthuse about the ultra-thin and crispy bases of the pizzas cooked by bakers who deftly flick the dough on to the hot oven floor and know exactly when to take it out.

Many restaurants, not just pizzerias, are now embracing the wood-fired oven, installing them in their own kitchens. Not

only do chefs enjoy the ability to cook food incredibly quickly with maximum flavour, but the customers love the drama of seeing their food disappearing into the flames and coming out moments later.

This kind of cooking might seem like something best left to the professionals, but it is the most immediate cooking experience you can get – and once you have learned about managing the fire and its temperatures, there is nothing you can't cook in your wood-fired oven.

One of the joys of using a wood-fired oven is the social aspect of it. Once your family and friends know about your oven, they'll be inviting themselves over to enjoy your incredible food as well as the drama of the oven itself. After cooking for

▼ *The best pizza restaurants always have the indoor wood-fired oven burning.*

them, you can then get them involved (in fact it's difficult to stop them), so cooking becomes an experience to share.

This book gives you all the practical help you need to make the most of your oven. It will take you through the basic steps of siting your oven to building and managing your fire. It covers every kind of cooking, from 90-second utterly thin and crispy pizzas to slow, leisurely overnight melt-in-the-mouth braises that squeeze every second out of the fire's falling temperatures and there are recipes for all the different ways of cooking in your oven. Having a wood-fired oven is the culinary adventure of a lifetime, and this book will support you every step of the way.

YOUR OVEN

Wood-fired ovens are flexible and adaptable, so think about what you want to use it for and what size of oven you need before you commit to building or buying one, to make sure you get the one that is just right for you. Positioning and structure are also very important, as is the finished look of the oven.

Wood-fired ovens can produce an intense, fierce heat or a more gentle, forgiving heat. The heat is produced in two ways:
• The primary heat is produced from the fire built inside the oven and is used for quick cooking (eg pizzas, fish, steaks, kebabs). The heat from the fire swirls around the dome-shaped roof, producing heat that cooks the food from all angles.
• The secondary heat is produced later by the bricks absorbing the heat from the flames and then slowly releasing this residual heat to cook dishes at lower temperatures. The heat is absorbed into the oven walls or thermal mass and is slowly released even after the fire has died down. It will continue cooking dishes but at lower temperatures.

CHOOSING THE RIGHT OVEN
Wood-fired ovens come in a variety of sizes and designs, and you will need to think about how you will use the oven and how many people you will be cooking for before choosing the appropriate one.
• If you like entertaining and often host a large number of friends, then you probably need a medium-large oven.
• If you think you are more likely to use the oven as an extension of your domestic kitchen, baking bread for the family and producing regular meals in it, then you

won't need more than a small-medium oven. A smaller oven will use less fuel and will heat up more quickly.

Check with your chosen supplier that the oven you are planning to buy will fulfil your expectations. It's a good idea to see how the oven works before you have one installed, by going on a course to find out how best to use it.

SMOKE CONTROL REGULATIONS
Some areas are subject to smoke control laws. Check with your local planning office to make sure that your plans for building or buying an oven don't contravene these laws. Your oven supplier will know whether your oven will pass these tests.

▲ Our own oven is built on decking, so we can use it all year. It is covered with a roof to keep out the worst of the weather.

SITING AND CONSTRUCTION
Spend some time thinking about where to build your oven. It is best to position it close to your own domestic kitchen. Consider the wood-fired oven area an extension of the house – if your wood-fired oven is easy to get to, whatever the weather, then you are much more likely to use it all year round. Our wood-fired oven is about 5m/16ft from the house and is at the end of some decking, so it's always dry underfoot, and a canvas roof means we are always under cover.

▼ This brick oven is well protected from the weather and has a good storage area underneath for logs.

▼ This oven has a tile roof for protection. The chimney has also been covered to stop any rain getting inside the oven.

▼ Even a small oven like this, without insulation or cladding, can reach high temperatures and cook excellent pizzas.

▲ *This oven is well insulated with a layer of bricks. The table close by is really useful for ingredients while cooking.*

Once you have decided where to site the oven, you will need a stand for it. Wood-fired ovens are heavy, so your stand will need to be able to support its weight – ours is made out of breeze blocks with iron struts running between them to prevent the walls from bowing. On top of the iron struts are some scaffolding planks, cut to size, and on top of them two large paving slabs, about 5cm/2in thick. Finally, on top of all of this is a 5cm/2in layer of sharp sand. This ensures a snug fit and insulation from beneath.

The stand for the oven should be about 1.2m/4ft off the floor so you can see easily into the oven through the door. Shelves underneath or to the side of the stand are useful for kindling and utensils.

Confirm with your builders' merchant or home improvement store that the materials you are using to construct the stand, oven surround and cladding are right for the job and will withstand the high heat produced by the oven.

FINISHING

For the best use of your oven, you should consider cladding it with insulation and covering it to protect it from the weather. Insulating the oven is critical for fuel use, as a well-insulated oven will use less wood to feed the fire and will reach the temperature you want more quickly. A wooden roof will keep the worst of the weather off the oven roof and the insulating materials. You will need a space between the wooden roof and the top of the oven and insulation so that there is easy access to the oven. A dry oven will be ready to cook in a much quicker time than a wet one, in which the fire will be using lots of energy to dry out the wet surroundings before it starts to cook.

Another addition you should think about is a flue extension to the chimney, which carries any smoke away from the house. A longer chimney also helps in other ways – it gives a greater draw of oxygen, which makes it easier to light the fire, and it also means that once it is lit, the fire will burn to a higher temperature more quickly.

On top of the flue, you should place a cowl, which prevents rain from coming down the chimney into the oven, keeping it dry and easy to light. This can also be angled to prevent smoke, heat and odours from wafting towards the house or your neighbours.

If you have it, allow plenty of space for logs, peels and utensils around your oven. A selection of pots of herbs to cook with are great to have close to hand.

Finishing your oven surrounds can be done in a variety of ways, either painting it or cladding it in brick, slate or stone.

▼ *This whitewashed oven, in a sunny spot in the garden, is sheltered from the weather by high walls.*

INSULATION

We have built some wooden walls around our oven, and into this space we have put ceramic fibre insulation. It is easy to reach the insulating material, in order to lift it up and take the temperature of the outside of the oven – useful for seeing if the thermal mass has heated through. You can also use other insulating materials such as sheep's wool.

DRYING AND SEASONING

Once you have finished building your oven or got your ready-made one into its final resting place, you need to ensure it is dried out and seasoned prior to cooking in it. The cement or mortar you have used in the construction needs to dry out as for any brick or concrete building. Once the oven is dry you then need to season it, so that the high heat of the baking temperatures doesn't cause the new oven to crack. Even ready-built ovens should be seasoned to drive off residual moisture.

To season your oven, you simply need to light a series of small fires inside the oven, allowing each fire to gradually build up to a temperature of about 200°C/400°F, then letting it die down. Do this three or four times before you start cooking in the oven. You will see the colour inside lightening as it dries out.

▼ *Grow lots of pots of herbs by the oven. Freshly picked for your recipes they add a burst of fresh, intense flavour.*

TOOLS AND EQUIPMENT

You don't need a huge number of special tools for your oven, but some are essential. This is what we recommend you have before you begin cooking. You can buy sets of tools quite easily, or you may be the kind of person who can fashion your own. The important thing is that what you use is safe, fireproof and will protect you from the heat.

Long-handled peels, gauntlets and a heat-proof thermometer are probably the most important pieces of equipment, without which you really shouldn't start to cook in your oven.

PEELS

These are long-handled, flat shovels used for moving food around the base of the oven and bringing cooked dishes toward the oven door so you don't have to reach in and run the risk of burning yourself. You can also use them to move burning logs.

It is useful to have three peels, all about 1m/3ft long:
- a wooden peel
- a small metal peel
- a large metal peel

Use a wooden peel for putting uncooked bread into the oven and for reaching in to take the bread out once it is cooked. The wood is gentler on the dough and bread – it is less likely than a

metal peel to cut into the uncooked dough. You can use a metal peel for putting bread into the oven and taking it out, although it is more likely to stick to the dough than a wooden one.

Use a metal peel for moving dishes around the oven if you want to move them to a cooler or hotter site. You can also use them for bringing dishes toward the oven door so you don't have to reach into the oven when it's hot. A metal peel is easier to insert under a metal dish in the oven than a wooden one, so you're less likely to tip over your dish if you can deftly insert the peel beneath it.

You can also use a metal peel to move the fire toward the back of the oven once it has reached the temperature you need for cooking – useful if you don't have a coal hook. It is handy but not essential to have a selection of peels of different sizes, as this makes it easier to manoeuvre dishes of different sizes.

COAL HOOK

This is a long metal pole with a hook on the end. It is used for moving the fire or embers around the oven once the heat has reached the correct temperature. It is also useful for pushing fresh logs on to the fire if you need to build up the heat again during cooking. Finally, once the fire has finished, you can use it for bringing the ashes toward the oven door so you can brush them out.

BRUSH

A long-handled brush, with metal bristles – usually copper – is a very practical tool for use in the wood-fired oven. Use it for brushing ash off the oven floor once you have moved the fire to the back of the oven and before you begin cooking straight on to the oven floor. It is also useful for brushing off any food that has spilled on to the oven floor during cooking and for brushing the cold ash out

▼ *You will need two or three metal peels, a wire brush, and a coal hook.*

▼ *Make the most of the space under your oven by adding hooks to hang your tools.*

▼ *A wooden peel is better than metal for pizza, as the dough is less likely to stick.*

of the oven door. Have a metal bucket handy by the oven door to brush the ashes into; you can then use them on the garden as potash or put them on the compost heap. As with the peels and the coal hook, the brush needs a long handle so you can reach in and around the oven easily without having to lean into the heat.

GAUNTLETS

It is a wise precaution to have a pair of long-sleeved thick gauntlets to wear when you are baking in the oven. The long sleeves will protect your arms from the intense heat, and individual gloves give you more freedom to move your hands independently than a pair of joined-up oven gloves. Even if your gauntlets are thick, it's worth using an oven cloth to give yourself some added protection when you are removing dishes from the oven until you get used to the heat.

THERMOMETER

A laser thermometer is the best way of taking the temperatures inside and outside the oven. Hold it outside the oven and direct the laser to the spot where you want to establish the temperature. You can see the different temperatures around the inside of the oven very quickly, so you can move a dish around to a cooler or hotter spot as needed.

▼ *A laser thermometer is very useful as it will read the temperature of all the different parts of the oven.*

▲ *Make sure you have a pair of thick, flame-retardant gauntlets that will protect your arms as well as your hands.*

A laser thermometer is also useful for establishing the heat on the outside of the oven, by aiming it at the external dome you can see that the thermal mass inside is building up.

A traditional oven thermometer can also be useful, as it will tell you the air temperature in the oven, which will always be less than the walls. However, do not use it in a roaring fire, as its gauge won't read the high temperatures of the oven and the glass face is likely to blacken or even crack in the high heat.

Some ovens have thermometers built into the outside of the oven wall so you can see the temperature inside the oven. However, the temperatures vary at different locations within the oven, and the laser thermometer gives you much more ability and speed to find the hot and cooler spots in your oven.

AXE

Get yourself a good solid axe to split the logs up into kindling so that you can start the fire more easily. Use it to split large logs into smaller sections so that they burn quicker and produce lots of heat. Split logs along the grain, not across it.

Use a large wooden block (in fact, a large section of a tree trunk) to split the

logs on. Store the axe by sticking it into the block when not in use, so you know where it is, and the blade isn't exposed. If you store the wood and the chopping block right by your oven, you won't have to carry heavy loads of wood back and forth when you're getting ready to build the fire and use the oven.

▼ *Keep a sharp axe and a supply of seasoned wood close to the oven, so kindling can be produced when needed.*

▲ *Enamel, copper, stainless steel and cast iron pots and pans will all withstand the high heat of the wood-fired oven.*

OVENWARE

In the wood-fired oven, use ovenware that will withstand very high temperatures. Also, try to make sure your ovenware is quite thick and sturdy so that the bases and sides don't warp or crack in the heat. The best ovenware to use is cast iron, as it will never warp, even at very high temperatures. Thick cast-iron pots and pans with tight-fitting lids are perfect for

▼ *Wire racks used for cooling cakes and loaves can also be used in the oven.*

use in the wood-fired oven – just remember they are heavy to lift in and out of the oven. You can also use metal-handled pans and frying pans with tight-fitting lids. Don't use anything with a wood handle or a plastic knob on the lid.

It is advisable to have a variety of heavy, metal roasting pans of different sizes and baking sheets to use for cooking at high heat. Additionally, enamelware and terracotta pots are useful for

▼ *Seasoning your pots means there will be no breakages and spills when you cook.*

SEASONING CLAY POTS

You can season terracotta or clay pots before baking in them, to make them non-stick and prevent any cracking once in the oven.
1 Brush the insides of the dishes with a little sunflower oil.
2 Place in a cold oven and build up a fire until the temperature reaches 200°C/400°F.
3 Let the fire gradually cool down with the pots still inside the oven until it is quite cold.
4 Oil and heat the pots twice more before baking in them.

slow-cooking. Seasoned terracotta or clay pots are generally thick enough to withstand high temperatures, but if you're not sure, just check with your supplier that they will survive in a wood-fired oven.

Pots and pans should be washed in warm soapy water, which will clean most of them. If anything is really sticking on the inside of the pan, leaving it to soak will help loosen it – usually, overnight is fine. If that still doesn't work, boil some water in it with a teaspoon or two of bicarbonate of soda, which will shift almost anything.

Wash metal baking sheets or roasting pans in hot, soapy water, and once they are clean, rub a little vegetable oil over them with a piece of kitchen paper, which should stop rust from forming.

USING THE RIGHT FUEL

Building a fire, lighting it successfully, and controlling the heat so that you can cook with it, is actually very easy, and is more to do with experimenting and experience than anything else. There are, however, a few guidelines, which will help you get it right sooner rather than later.

The most important thing to consider when lighting your oven is using the right fuel. You need to use wood that is well seasoned and has been dried out over a period of about two years in a dry place away from rain so the natural moisture – the sap – in the wood has gone. Kiln-dried wood is often recommended for wood-fired ovens, but it is expensive and humans have been using seasoned wood for thousands of years perfectly happily without drying it in a kiln.

If you are buying wood from a wood merchants, ask how long the wood has

▲ *Find a local wood supplier who can provide well-seasoned hard wood logs.*

▲ *Split the logs lengthways to get thin kindling, which is essential to start the fire.*

SAFETY TIPS

- Use gauntlets and wear sturdy shoes, not sandals
- Wear long, close-fitting sleeves
- Keep a bucket of sand or water close to the fire while it is lit
- Make sure there is nothing highly combustible near the oven door
- Never use treated timber in your oven as it may release toxins

▼ *Keep a pile of split logs close to the oven for feeding the fire as it builds up.*

been stored, what the water percentage is and what type of wood is in stock. If you say you are using the wood to burn in a wood-fired oven, they should be able to help you with specific information. If they can't tell you the moisture percentage of the wood, then it's probably a good idea to go elsewhere.

The wood should be cut roughly 25cm/10in long so that it fits conveniently in the oven. You need a mixture of thin logs for adding to your pile of burning kindling or quickly building up heat, and thicker ones for longer burning.

Store your wood in a weather-proof shed or stacked up and under some kind of shelter so that it stays dry. Air is necessary to help keep the wood dry, so don't cover the wood with a tarpaulin as this will inhibit circulation.

LOGS
The best types of wood to use are hard, slow-burning ones that release a lot of heat such as oak, beech, ash, birch and olive. Don't use pine logs, as they will spit aggressively and the resin will release lots of black smoke on burning. This resinous smoke will also give an unpleasant flavour to the food. Pine smoke will also produce a lot of soot that, over time, will clog up your oven's chimney. Avoid using broken up wooden pallets, and other treated wood such as fence posts, because they will release chemical toxins on burning.

KINDLING
It is essential to have small dry pieces of wood to start a fire. Keep a box or two under cover by the side of the oven so you can use it at a moment's notice, together with old newspapers and a box or two of long matches.

Use either bundles of dry twigs or fir cones that you have collected from the garden or some of the logs used on the fire split down into small pieces lengthways. Your kindling shouldn't be much thicker than a twig, so use your axe to split logs into kindling on your wooden block, 1cm/½in thick.

GATHERING WOOD YOURSELF

- First of all, make sure you have permission from the landowner, and always make sure you are not disturbing any wildlife
- Only use wood that is already lying on the ground or from dead trees – never strip branches from live trees
- Make sure it is hard wood, not pine
- Use a sharp saw to cut branches into manageable pieces or to cut large logs into the lengths you want
- Stack the wood raised above the ground in a dry place to season; it needs to be under cover but with the ends exposed so air can circulate and moisture escape.

LIGHTING AND CONTROLLING A FIRE

To build your fire you will need several well-seasoned hardwood split logs, cut to about 25cm/10in in length, and of varying thicknesses, thin ones to begin with and thicker ones for once the flames are established. You will also need a pile of dry split kindling, about 2cm/1in thick, some scrunched up newspaper and matches.

LIGHTING A FIRE

1 Take three logs and make an open-fronted 'hearth' near the front of your oven. This will hold the fire together in its early stages. Having the fire near the door provides the maximum amount of oxygen in its early stages.

2 Tightly scrunch up four or five sheets of newspaper and put on the base of the oven floor inside your 'hearth'.

3 Place some of the smallest pieces of kindling over the newspaper with some thicker sticks on top at right angles. Leave small gaps between each piece of wood to allow the flames to rise through them.

4 Light the newspaper and let the kindling catch. Firelighters can be used, but doing without is good practice, easy after a bit of practice, and more satisfying.

5 When the kindling and thicker sticks are burning well, add four or five fairly thin split logs on the top and leave to catch. Wear a pair of gauntlet-style gloves to protect your hands when doing this.

6 Keep adding thicker logs to gradually increase the temperature, but don't add too much fuel. The oven will only absorb energy at a certain rate, so a medium-size fire will heat just the inside of the oven just as quickly as a large one.

7 Once the fire is well established, push it to the back or side of the oven. Put the door in front of the entrance but leave it slightly ajar to draw in the air.

8 Use a laser thermometer to test the oven temperature. Take the temperature of the roof, walls and floor of the oven to give an overall picture of the heat.

9 If you are going to cook something quickly, such as fish or pizzas, then you are ready to cook as the oven floor reaches the temperature you want.

10 If you want a prolonged heat for longer cooking without flames, you will need to heat the entire thermal mass of the oven, If possible, take the external temperature of the oven, then compare this to the inside temperature. Initially there will be a large differential, but the two temperatures will become closer as you heat the oven for longer.

11 If you are cooking straight on the floor of the oven, use a long-handled fireproof brush to sweep ash from the oven floor.

MAINTAINING THE FIRE AND TEMPERATURE

1 To maintain the fire at the temperature you want, keep testing the temperature and add wood, one log at a time, as the temperature drops, to build it back up.

2 Once the oven has reached the temperature you want, keep the door closed to keep the heat inside, unless you wish to continue cooking with the flames burning. If you are cooking something very quickly, such as pizzas, pitta breads or fish fillets, you can leave the door open so you can keep an eye on the food. Shutting the door starves the fire of oxygen, so leave the door ajar if you want to keep the flames burning.

DROPPING THE TEMPERATURE

The temperature in the oven will drop naturally once the fire has died down, but if you want to drop the temperature more quickly you can:

1 Leave the door open to encourage the heat to come out of the door.

2 Sweep the base of your oven with a wet dish towel attached to a metal peel.

3 Rake over the embers with a coal hook to spread them into a single layer, rather than leaving them in a bank, which will retain the heat longer.

RAISING THE TEMPERATURE

1 If you want to raise the temperature in the oven, add more kindling and smaller logs to the fire, pushing them on to the flames with a coal hook.

2 Close the oven door, leaving it slightly ajar, and let the heat build up until the oven is at the temperature you need.

FLAMES OR EMBERS?

A flaming fire will act as a grill, great for intense heat all over, good for sizzling cheese on a pizza or searing steaks. Only quick-cook dishes can be cooked in a blazing fire.

A slow-burning fire will add smokiness to longer-cooked dishes like roast chicken, and is great for kebabs, whole fish or roast potatoes.

Glowing embers are great for slow-roasting a joint of meat, while for breads and cakes a raked out oven with an all-round heat is best.

FINISHING AND CLEANING

1 When the fire is out and completely cold, use a coal hook or peel to drag out any charcoal or ashes. You could put it on a compost heap, if you have one.

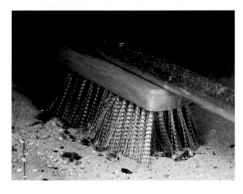

2 Use a metal brush to rub any ingredients off the base of the oven if they have fallen on it during cooking, making sure the oven is clean for its next use.

▼ *Once you master the art of starting, building and managing the fire to high enough temperatures, you will be able to successfuly cook a huge range of dishes.*

MENU IDEAS AND TIMING GUIDES

Once you have got to grips with how your oven works, you can use it to cook a whole variety of dishes, and use the heat you've created to the absolute maximum. Use the following time plan suggestions as a guideline for some delicious meals and parties, but feel free to experiment with your own selection of recipes.

- English muffins
- Frittata verde
- Slow-roasted tomatoes with herbs
- Bacon and sausages

BREAKFAST

A leisurely breakfast or brunch is one of the nicest ways of using your wood-fired oven, and if you have a weekend house party, or family gathering, it's a great way to bring everyone together at the beginning of the day.

Time plan for a 10am brunch
8am Make and knead the dough for the muffins and leave to rise. Light the fire.
9.15am Turn the dough into muffins. Prepare the tomatoes, and when the oven has reached 190°C/375°F put in the coolest area.
9.30am Put the sausages in a roasting pan and place in the oven. Put the vegetables for the frittata in an ovenproof dish and place that in the oven too.
9.45am Put the muffins in the oven. Mix the eggs for the frittata into the vegetables, finish the recipe and place the pan in the oven.

9.50am Put the rashers of bacon on a baking sheet or metal-handled frying pan in the hottest part of the oven.
9.55am Check the muffins, and when cooked, remove to a wire tray and cover with a clean dish towel. The frittata, sausages and slow-roasted tomatoes should also be cooked by now, so take them out and put them on a trivet on the table.
10am Take out the bacon, when it is cooked to your liking, sit everyone down, and serve everything on warmed plates, along with orange juice, tea and coffee.

- Fish soup with aioli and sourdough toasts
- Lemon and thyme roasted chicken with wilted greens
- Potatoes Provençal
- Olive oil cake with nectarines and raspberries

LONG SUMMER LUNCH

Al fresco eating doesn't get better than a long lunch with friends in your garden (backyard) or on your decking. These menus are all planned for a one o'clock lunch, but if you want to eat later, just put the timings back.

Time plan for a 1pm lunch
8.30am Light the fire, and build it up to 190°C/375°F.
9.30am Prepare the chicken for the oven.
10am Put the chicken in the oven to roast. Prepare the olive oil cake.
10.30am Start cooking the vegetables for the tomato sauce for the soup in the coolest part of oven.
10.45am Add the rest of the ingredients to the sauce and return to the oven.
11am Take the tomato sauce out of the oven and whizz up. Put the olive oil cake in the oven. Prepare the potatoes Provençal.
11.40am Put the potatoes Provençal in the oven. Take the cake out of the oven if it's ready, and turn out to cool on a wire rack.
Noon Take the foil off the chicken and put the bird back in the oven to brown the skin.
12.15pm Put the tomato sauce and all of the soup base ingredients into the oven. Make the aioli for the fish soup and chill until needed. Chop the greens.
12.50pm Take the chicken out of the oven and leave it to rest in a warm place. Put the

fish and spinach in the soup base to cook.
12.55pm Put the toasts in the oven to grill.
1pm Take the fish soup and toasts out of the oven and serve with the aioli. Put the chopped greens in the oven to wilt while you are eating the soup.
1.10pm Carve the chicken. Take the potatoes and the vegetables out of the oven and serve with the chicken. Once you have finished the chicken, you can serve up the olive oil cake, dusted with icing (confectioner's) sugar and accompanied by whipped cream.

ITALIAN SUNDAY LUNCH

The Italians really know how to create al fresco feasts, and of course getting the family sitting down together for a meal on a Sunday is very much part of Italian tradition.

- Monkfish and prawn skewers with coriander salsa
- Bistecca Fiorentina
- Rocket (arugula) salad
- Mini roast potatoes
- Pear and almond open tart with crème fraîche

Time plan for a 1pm lunch
10.30am Heat the oven to 200°C/400°F. Prepare the pear and almond tart, and set aside. Prepare the fish and prawns (shrimp) for the skewers and leave to marinate.
11.45am Place the tart in the oven.
Noon When cooked, take the tart out of the oven and leave to cool. Build the fire up until it reaches 250°C/480°F.
12.15pm Make the coriander salsa. Prepare the potatoes in the roasting pans. Get the bistecca ready for the oven.
12.30pm Thread the fish and prawns on to metal skewers.
12.45pm Put the potatoes in the oven until golden, roasted and tender.
12.55pm Put the fish skewers in the oven.

1pm Take the skewers out of the oven. Put the bistecca in the oven for 10–12 minutes. While it cooks, serve the fish skewers with the salsa.
1.12pm Take the bistecca out of the oven. Leave, covered, in a warm place for 5–10 minutes.
1.35pm Take the potatoes out of the oven and place them on the table. Toss some baby rocket (arugula) and spinach with a squeeze of lemon juice and some peppery olive oil. Season well.
   Carve the bistecca at the table and serve with the salad and the potatoes and any meat juices left in the pan.
2.30pm Serve the tart, when you are ready, with some crème fraîche and strong coffee.

SOPHISTICATED EVENING DINNER PARTY

The following are timings for menu ideas for an eight o'clock dinner. It's best to get as much of the preparation as possible done in advance, as well as some of the cooking – then you'll have time to get ready for when your friends arrive, and you're ready to put things in the oven.

- Scallops with chilli and mint
- Ciabatta
- Roast venison with prosciutto
- Roast squash and sweet potato mash with chilli, garlic and thyme
- Braised red cabbage with red wine and pears
- Plum and blackberry crumble

Time plan for an 8pm dinner
Night before Make the biga for the ciabattas.
8am Start making the ciabattas. This will need 2½ hours of folding and relaxing to get them ready to go into the oven.
9am Build the fire to get to 230°C/450°F.
10.30am Bake the ciabattas.
10.50am Take the bread out of the oven and cool on wire racks.
   Allow the oven temperature to fall to around 200°C/400°F.
11am Prepare the plum and blackberry crumble for baking and set aside until later.
11.15am Bake the squash and sweet potatoes for the mash, but push them to the cooler part of the oven.
11.30am Prepare the braised red cabbage with red wine and pears for baking.
Noon When the oven has fallen to 150°C/300°F, put the red cabbage in.
12.15pm Take out the squash and sweet potatoes and make the mash. Put into a serving dish that you can reheat later.
   Prepare the scallops and the venison for baking, but keep them in the refrigerator on a baking sheet.
2pm Check the cabbage and, if ready, take out of the oven. Close the oven door to keep the heat inside. Take the rest of the afternoon

off but keep the fire ticking over if you can to save time later.
6.30pm Take the scallops and venison out of the refrigerator to bring them to room temperature. Build the fire up to 250°C/480°F.
7.30pm Wrap the dishes of red cabbage and mash in a double layer of foil each and put them in the coolest part of the oven to gradually warm up.
7.55pm Bake the scallops in the oven for 5 minutes, warm the ciabattas at the same time, if you wish.
8pm Remove the scallops from the oven and serve with the ciabattas. Put the venison in the oven to roast for 10 minutes.
8.10pm Take the venison out of the oven and allow to rest for 10 minutes covered with some foil. Make the gravy. Let the temperature in the oven drop to 190°C/375°F.
8.20pm Take the mash and the red cabbage out of the oven. Carve the venison, garnish with the parsley and serve with the mash, cabbage and gravy.
8.30pm Put the crumble in the oven to bake.
9pm Take the crumble out of the oven and keep warm until you are ready to serve it. Dust with icing (confectioners') sugar and serve with ice cream, vanilla custard or clotted cream.

- Stuffed red (bell) peppers with pine nuts and oregano
- Focaccia
- Porchetta
- White beans with sage and garlic
- Mixed leaf and herb salad with toasted pumpkin seeds
- Roast peaches with amaretti, served with crème fraîche

EASY EVENING SUPPER PARTY

This menu has an Italian feel – it's colourful and full of flavour with lots of contrasting textures. It's perfect for a leisurely supper with friends and family sitting in the warmth of a summer evening. The preparation and cooking can all be done beforehand so you can concentrate on spending time with your guests. If you cook double the peppers and two pieces of pork, then there will be plenty of leftovers for the next day.

Time plan for an 8pm dinner

Night before Place the white beans in a large bowl covered with plenty of cold water and leave to soak overnight. Make the biga for the focaccia.

9am Make the dough for the focaccia. This will need about 2½ hours of folding and resting until it's ready for the oven.

10.30am Build the fire in the oven so that it reaches 250°C/480°F. Prepare the white beans, porchetta, red (bell) peppers with pine nuts, and the roast peaches, for baking, but don't put them in the oven just yet. Keep the porchetta in the refrigerator until you're ready for it to go in the oven.

11.30am Bake the focaccia.

11.45am Take the focaccia out of the oven when they are ready, and cool on a wire rack. Allow the oven to fall to 200°C/400°F.

Noon Place the peaches and the peppers in the oven. Put 45ml/3 tbsp of pumpkin seeds in a ovenproof frying pan and toast in the oven for 5–6 minutes until golden brown.

12.30pm Take the peaches and peppers out of the oven when both are tender, and leave to cool at room temperature. Cover and, when cool, put in the refrigerator. Let the oven fall to 150°C/300°F.

4pm Boil the beans vigorously on the stove for 10 minutes.

4.10pm Cover the beans and put them in the oven to bake slowly. Build the fire up until it reaches 150°C/300°F if it has fallen during the afternoon.

5pm Put the porchetta in the oven to roast slowly. Stir the beans.

7pm Take the peppers and the peaches out of the refrigerator to come to room temperature.

7.30pm Test the beans to make sure they are tender. If soft, season with salt and pepper. Put back in the oven to keep warm.

8pm Serve the peppers, drizzled with a little olive oil, along with the focaccia. Take the meat out of the oven to rest.

8.30pm Make the salad by mixing 4 large handfuls of mixed baby leaves with a few tablespoons of fresh herbs such as basil, coriander (cilantro), lemon balm and a little thyme. Squeeze over the juice of a lemon, drizzle over some peppery olive oil, season with salt and pepper and sprinkle over a few of the pumpkin seeds that you toasted earlier.

8.40pm Serve the porchetta in thick slices, with the white beans and salad.

9.30pm Serve the roast peaches.

- White bloomer with poppy seeds
- Simple white sourdough loaf
- Clay pot loaf
- Multi-seeded wholemeal and spelt loaf with honey
- Bannock
- Apple pie with spices
- Upside-down rhubarb and ginger cake
- Chocolate brownies
- Rich fruit cake
- Meringues

> **COOK'S TIP**
> Drink lots of water while you are working, as baking close to a hot oven all day can cause dehydration.

WOOD-FIRED OVEN BAKING DAY

Bread needs high temperatures, so you have to build up the fire in advance. To make the most of the heat produced, set aside some time to bake a whole range of treats that will keep either in the freezer or in air-tight tins. The ideal way to bake is to fire the oven over a period of time until the entire thermal mass is heated through to about 230°C/450°F. Then rake out the fire, leave for 20–30 minutes for the temperature to stabilize and then start baking.

Time plan for a baking day

3 days before Mix the starter for the sourdough loaves if you haven't got one on the go.

Night before Soak the fruit for the fruit cake.

7am Make the doughs for the sourdough, bloomer, clay pot and wholemeal and spelt loaves. Knead and set to prove as in each of the recipes.

10am Build the fire up to 230°C/450°F.

10.30am Rake out the embers and leave the oven to stabilize.

11am–1pm Bake the loaves in the oven as

they are ready. As the loaves are cooked, cool them on wire racks.

1pm Clear up and have some lunch while letting the oven temperature drop to around 200°C/400°F.

1.30pm Make the dough for the bannocks and bake in the oven. Cook the apples for the pie in the coolest part of the oven. Take out when they are ready, in 10–12 minutes. Set aside to cool.

2pm Take the bannocks out of the oven if they are ready. Make up the apple pie and bake in the oven.

COOK'S TIP

All these delicious breads and cakes can be frozen, either whole or cut into slices, apart from meringues, which can be stored in an airtight container.

2.30–2.40pm Take the apple pie out when it's ready and cool. Let the oven drop to around 180°C/350°F. Make up the upside-down rhubarb and ginger cake and the chocolate brownies. Put them in the cooler oven when they are ready. Mix up the rich fruit cake.
3–3.15pm Take the brownies out of the oven, check the rhubarb and ginger cake, and remove that when cooked. Let the oven drop

to 140°C/275°F before putting in the rich fruit cake.
5.15pm Mix up the meringues. Check the fruit cake to see if it's ready.
6.30pm When the oven has fallen to 100°C/200°F put in the meringues. Bake for 2 hours, or overnight. Clear up and have a cup of tea while surveying your baking marathon. Time to put your feet up and taste the results!

PIZZA PARTY

There's nothing like a pizza party to bring the generations together. Make up the dough, get the sauce made, have a variety of toppings for everyone to choose from and let the party begin. Make double or triple the amount of dough and sauce and you can cook for a crowd. Make sure you have plenty of fine ground semolina so the pizzas don't stick to the peel, a sharp knife to chop them up, and plenty of paper napkins.

Time plan for a 6pm party
3.30pm Light the fire, build the temperature until the oven reaches 150°C/300°F.
4pm Make the dough and leave to rise.
4.30pm Put the vegetables for the tomato sauce in the oven to become tender. Make the pizza dough and leave it to rise.
4.40pm Add the rest of the tomato sauce ingredients and finish cooking in the oven.
5pm Take the sauce out of the oven. Blend

until smooth and leave to cool. Build the fire in the oven up to reach 450°C/840°F. Prepare your the toppings and arrange on plates.
5.50pm Divide the dough into 150g/5oz balls.
6pm Get everyone to make their own pizzas, including rolling or spinning the dough to get the base. Start cooking and eating. Keep an eye on the temperature of the oven and maintain the right heat by adding one or two fairly slender logs at a time, as necessary.

Toppings you might like to prepare could include the following:
• thinly sliced red onions
• red and yellow (bell) peppers
• thinly sliced mushrooms
• sliced tomatoes
• flaked tuna
• drained anchovies
• drained capers
• pitted olives
• thinly sliced cured meats, such as pepperoni, chorizo, salami and Parma ham
• mozzarella, torn into pieces
• grated strong-flavoured cheeses, such as Parmesan and Cheddar

- Chilli con carne
- Baked potatoes
- Cornbread
- Coleslaw
- Apple pie with spices

HOME ON THE RANGE

This is great to leave cooking while you are out – sailing, walking, riding, canoeing; whatever the activity, this meal will warm your crowd up when you return home tired and hungry. You can leave the chilli in the oven longer if you are running late.

Time plan for a 2pm lunch
8.30am Build the fire up to 230°C/450°F.
10am Start browning the meat for the chilli and, when done, let the temperature drop to 200°C/400°F. Prepare the cornbread and finish making the chilli.
10.30am Bake the cornbread. Put together the apple pie so that it's ready to bake, but don't put it in the oven yet.

Rustle up a coleslaw with a small finely chopped white cabbage, 2 grated carrots and apples and some mayonnaise and yogurt, salt and pepper. Put in the refrigerator.

11am Take the cornbread out of the oven and cool on a wire rack. Let the oven drop to 160°C/325°F and put the chilli and 6 large baking potatoes, pricked and wrapped in foil, in the oven. Take a break.
2pm Come back for lunch, but the chilli and potatoes will be fine in the oven, so don't worry if you're running late. Build the oven back up to 200°C/400°F and bake the apple pie for 25–30 minutes while you serve up the chilli, potatoes, cornbread and coleslaw.
3pm Serve the apple pie with some vanilla ice cream.

- Scallops with chilli and mint
- Marinated squid
- Spicy marinated pork ribs
- Lamb koftas with tomato salsa and pitta breads
- Jerk chicken
- Chilli and mint beef skewers
- Rosemary and sea-salt focaccia
- Mini chocolate brownies
- Mini meringues with cream and fresh berries

> **COOK'S TIP**
> Rather than use individual plates for this party, simply pile all the food on to big serving platters and supply your guests with piles of paper napkins and finger bowls.

FINGER FOOD FEAST

This is similar to the pizza party in that you can get all the preparation done in advance and then bake in the hot oven in sequence, handing the food round to your friends. Cut the food into small bites so that it is easier to eat with your fingers.

Time plan for a 7pm party
A day in advance Cook the brownies and mini meringues.
Night before Marinate the jerk chicken and pork ribs in separate bowls.
1pm Make the dough for the focaccia and the pitta breads and leave to rise, folding as necessary.
2pm Build up the fire until it reaches 350°C/660°F.
3pm Shape and bake the pitta breads and cover with a clean cloth when cooked. Let the oven temperature drop to 230°C/450°F. Prepare the squid, koftas, tomato salsa, beef skewers and scallops.
5pm Bake the focaccia.

6.30pm Cut the brownies into mini squares and pile on a plate. Sandwich the meringues together with whipped cream and arrange on a plate around a pile of fresh strawberries. Keep the desserts in the refrigerator until you are ready to whisk them out.
7pm When your friends arrive, or when you're ready to eat, put the breads and salsa on the table and then bake the food in batches, so that one dish is followed by another in a relaxed fashion. Try cooking the scallops and squid first, followed by each meat dish.
9pm After producing all the lovely succulent meat dishes from the oven, whisk the brownies and meringues out of the refrigerator and pass them round.

NIGHT BAKES

When you've used your oven, think ahead to how you can use its falling heat overnight, meaning you've got food for the next day without having to fire up the oven again.

All of the dishes on the right would work well in an overnight oven, possibly cooler than the recipe states, but that's fine – they will cook away happily until the morning. Obviously, you won't be able to get all of these in at the same time, but if you get into the habit of having something ready-prepared to pop in the oven to use up the residual heat, it does make a lot of sense in terms of saving fuel and time. Chicken stock can also be cooked overnight, see page 54.

- Cassoulet
- Boston baked beans
- Roast butternut squash for mash
- Kleftico
- Lamb and prune tagine
- Porchetta
- White beans with sage and garlic
- Red cabbage with red wine and pears
- Slow-roast tomatoes with herbs
- Meringues
- Breadcrumbs (Put stale bread in a roasting pan in the cool oven overnight. In the morning, whizz to crumbs in a food processor.)

COOKOUT WEEKENDS

Now you've got to grips with what you can do with your wood-fired oven you can plan to use it all weekend right through until Sunday evening. Here's a suggestion of what to cook during a weekend, although you can pretty much cook anything you want to fit in with your plans.

Friday Dinner
Braised sausages with leeks, apples and cider, served with baked potatoes and braised red cabbage
Fruit crumble served with cream
- Cook some caramelized shallots and a tray of red (bell) peppers overnight for pizza toppings the next day.

Saturday Breakfast
Bacon, eggs, mushrooms and tomatoes, served with toasted ciabatta rounds

Saturday Lunch
Pizzas
Bananas, baked in the oven in their skins, served with ice cream

Saturday Dinner
Wild mushroom risotto
Roast duck with orange, star anise and cinnamon, with roast potatoes, watercress and rocket salad

Roast peaches with amaretti
- Cook white beans with sage and garlic overnight to eat with porchetta the next day

Sunday Brunch
Bannock with smoked salmon and
Poached eggs or bacon and fried eggs with English muffins and oven-roasted tomatoes
- Bake upside-down rhubarb and ginger cake in the falling oven, ready for tea later.

Sunday Afternoon Tea
Frittata verde
Upside-down rhubarb and ginger cake

Sunday Dinner
Porchetta with white beans cooked overnight
Baby spinach salad with herbs
Mini brownies with fresh strawberries and vanilla ice cream
- Just before you go to bed, put meringues in the cooling oven for storing in airtight containers for the week ahead.

ADAPTING RECIPES FOR THE WOOD-FIRED OVEN

Pretty much every recipe can be cooked in the wood-fired oven successfully. For a recipe cooked in a conventional oven, build your fire to the recommended temperature, then make the dish as normal. Check it 5 minutes before the cooking time is done. If it's a dish usually cooked on the stove, like fish soup on page 40, then break it down into the different stages – and simply adapt it to the oven. You can also half adapt recipes; if you want to put a casserole, like chilli on page 56, in a falling oven, make it up on the stove top in your kitchen as you usually do, and then just put it in the oven when it falls to the right temperature. This makes multiple-dish meals much easier.

PIZZAS

For many people pizzas are the best or even the only reason for getting a wood-fired oven. No domestic oven can ever replicate the intense heat of the oven floor combined with the grilling effect of a hot fire running over the pizzas. Add to this smoky flavours from the fire and you have a pizza which transports you straight back to that place in Naples where you ate the best pizza you ever had. An evening around the oven making pizzas is a great way to spend time with family or friends.

PIZZA DOUGH

This is a very straightforward dough, which makes five or six thin, crispy pizzas with a diameter of 30cm/12in. Use this basic dough for all the recipes in this chapter. If you don't want to use all of the pizza dough at one time, roll out and par-bake the rest to make pizza bases for future use – they are easy to stack and freeze like this.

1 Mix the yeast with half the water in a small bowl, and stir to get a smooth liquid. Sift the flour and the salt together into a large bowl.

2 Pour the yeast and water mixture on to the flour, then add the rest of the water and the olive oil. Use your hand, or a wooden spoon, to mix to a soft dough.

3 Transfer the dough on to a work surface – you don't need to put any extra flour on it, as this would cause the dough to slide around.

4 Knead the dough vigorously for about 10 minutes, until smooth, shiny and elastic. It is important to develop a really strong and stretchy dough that will then allow you to make good thin bases.

5 Put the dough in a lightly oiled bowl, and cover with a plastic bag. Leave in a warm place for about 60 minutes, until roughly doubled in size.

6 Tip the dough out and reknead briefly. Cut into five equal pieces and shape into balls. At this stage you can put the balls into the refrigerator to make pizzas later, if you wish.

7 Use a rolling pin to roll out each ball to rounds of 25cm/10in and about 3mm/⅛in thick. If you're feeling confident, pass the pizza dough from hand to hand, turning it as you go to make the rounds. However, be prepared to spend a little time getting your technique right. The pizza bases are now ready for a topping.

BAKING PIZZAS IN A WOOD-FIRED OVEN

The temperatures used for baking pizzas in the wood-fired oven are incredibly hot. It is this, however, that will make your pizzas so superior to those cooked in a conventional oven, with a crispy base and a topping that is slightly charred, with a smoky flavour, but still nice and moist because the cooking period is so short. You can leave the oven door open while cooking the pizzas, as the high heat won't disperse in the short time it takes to bake them and the fire needs a constant air supply to keep it burning. It doesn't matter if the flames are still high when you start cooking – as long as you push the fire to the back or side of the oven there will be plenty of space for the pizzas, and the flames add a good colouring and smoky flavour to the toppings. A fierce fire is perfect for pizzas.

When making up the pizzas, use reduced sauces and be careful not to overload the base with toppings, otherwise it may become heavy and soggy. Have all the toppings lined up and ready to go, especially if you are cooking lots of different pizzas for a large group.

Use plenty of fine ground semolina, this acts as tiny ball-bearings, and stops the uncooked base from sticking to the wooden peel. After you have cooked all of the pizzas, use the falling oven to slow-cook meat and vegetable dishes for later.

MAKES FIVE 25CM/10IN BASES

10g/¼oz fresh yeast
270ml/9½fl oz/1 scant cup warm
   water
450g/1lb/4 cups strong white
   bread flour
5ml/1 tsp salt
30ml/2 tbsp olive oil

PER PIZZA Energy 279kcal/1183kJ; Protein 9g; Carbohydrate 56g, of which sugars 1g; Fat 4g, of which saturates 1g; Cholesterol 0mg; Calcium 105mg; Fibre 2.8g; Sodium 985mg.

MAKES ENOUGH FOR 7–8 PIZZAS

15ml/1 tbsp olive oil
1 medium onion, finely chopped
1 small carrot, peeled and diced
1 stick celery, finely sliced
1 clove garlic, peeled and crushed
400g/14oz can chopped tomatoes
100ml/3½fl oz/scant ½ cup red or
   white wine
5ml/1 tsp dried herbes de Provence
salt and ground black pepper

FOR 2 30cm/11in PIZZAS
⅓ quantity pizza dough (page 24)
60ml/4 tbsp tomato sauce
60g/2oz mozzarella balls
fresh basil leaves
fine ground semolina, for sprinkling
olive oil for drizzling

PER PIZZA Energy 37kcal/153kJ; Protein 1g;
Carbohydrate 4g, of which sugars 3g; Fat 2g, of
which saturates 0g; Cholesterol 0mg; Calcium
21mg; Fibre 1.0g; Sodium 74mg.

TOMATO SAUCE PIZZA

This slow-cooked sauce can be used for all your tomato-based pizzas. It will make enough for seven or eight pizzas and will keep in the refrigerator or can be frozen if you don't use it all in one go. You can also use it for pasta and casseroles, so you may even want to make double the quantity and freeze in batches.

1 Build the fire in the oven until it is up to 150°C/300°F, this will take about 30 minutes. When it is up to temperature, push the fire to the back of the oven with a metal peel or coal hook. Keep the oven door closed to keep the heat inside.

2 Put the oil in an ovenproof pan and add the chopped onion, carrot, celery and garlic. Cover and cook in the oven with the door closed for 10 minutes, until the vegetables are starting to soften but not colour.

3 Remove the dish from the oven, using thick gauntlets or long oven gloves. Stir in the tomatoes, wine and herbs. Season with salt and pepper. Put the dish back in the oven with the lid on. Close the door and simmer for 15–20 minutes, until the vegetables are tender and the sauce has reduced.

4 Take the pan out of the oven, then transfer the sauce to a bowl or food processor.

5 Blend the sauce with a hand blender or processor until smooth. Cool before use, then chill until you are ready to use it on the pizzas, or freeze it in two or three batches.

6 To make the simplest of pizzas, build up the fire to a temperature of 400°C/750°F, this will take around 30 minutes. Sprinkle a wooden peel with fine ground semolina and place a dough round on top. Spread with a thin layer of tomato sauce, top with torn lumps of mozzarella and drizzle olive oil over the top.

7 Flick the pizza on to the floor of the oven. Cook for 90 seconds with the door open, until crisp and slightly charred. Remove with the peel and eat when slightly cooled.

½ quantity pizza dough (page 24)
1 small courgette (zucchini)
1 red or yellow (bell) pepper, cut in half and seeded
1 small aubergine (eggplant)
1 red onion
60ml/4 tbsp olive oil
30ml/2 tbsp fresh chopped oregano leaves
30ml/2 tbsp fresh chopped basil leaves
60ml/4 tbsp tomato sauce (page 25)
salt and ground black pepper
fine ground semolina, for sprinkling

VARIATION
Scatter the top of the pizza with a few cubes of goat's cheese, if you wish.

PER PIZZA Energy 668kcal/2790kJ; Protein 13g; Carbohydrate 73g, of which sugars 15g; Fat 38g, of which saturates 6g; Cholesterol 0mg; Calcium 173mg; Fibre 8.2g; Sodium 1032mg.

PIZZA WITH ROAST SUMMER VEGETABLES

Roasting brings out the sweetness of summer vegetables, such as courgettes, peppers and aubergines, and a combination of these, together with fresh herbs, makes a perfect pizza topping. The intense heat of the wood-fired oven chars the vegetables, so that they gain extra flavour while still remaining moist.

1 Build up the fire in the oven until it is about 190°C/375°F, this will take about 30 minutes. When it is up to temperature, push the fire to the back of the oven with a metal peel or coal hook, and close the oven door to keep the heat inside.

2 Chop the vegetables into pieces measuring about 2.5cm/1in. Put them in a large bowl and pour in the olive oil, mix with your hands so all the vegetables are coated in oil. Transfer to a large roasting pan and spread out in a single layer, using two pans if you need to. Roast the vegetables in the hot oven for around 20–30 minutes, stirring a couple of times, until the vegetables are tender but still hold their shape.

3 Take the roasting pans out of the oven, and set aside to cool down. When they are cool, toss through the chopped herbs and season well with salt and pepper.

4 Meanwhile, build up the fire on the base of the oven so that the temperature reaches 400°C/750°F. This will take about another 30 minutes. Push the fire to the back of the oven with a metal peel or coal hook.

5 Divide the pizza dough into two and roll out into rounds roughly 30cm/12in wide and 3mm/⅛in thick. Put a base on a peel sprinkled with plenty of fine ground semolina. This helps to prevent the dough from sticking to the surface.

6 Spread half the tomato sauce over the base, using the back of a tablespoon to spread it evenly. Leave a border of about 2.5cm/1in round the edge, so that the sauce doesn't spill when cooking. Scatter half of the roast vegetables on top.

7 Flick the first pizza on to the base of the oven, then assemble the second pizza.

8 Bake the pizzas on the oven floor for 90 seconds, with the door open, or until the bases are crispy and the toppings are charring and bubbling. Use a metal peel to turn the pizzas, so that the side nearest the flames doesn't char too much.

9 Use a peel to take the pizzas out of the oven and put them on a large wooden board. Allow the pizzas to set for a minute before cutting them into slices with a large, sharp knife. Eat straight away.

PIZZA FOCOSA

This pizza is perfect for chilli lovers. The beans add a great texture to the tomato sauce; white beans would work well if you haven't got any kidney beans.

1 Build up the fire in the oven until it is about 400°C/750°F, this will take about 60 minutes. When it is up to temperature, push the fire to the back of the oven with a metal peel or coal hook. Close the door to keep the heat inside.

2 Divide the pizza dough into two and roll out into rounds roughly 30cm/12in wide and 3mm/⅛in thick.

3 In a large bowl, use a potato masher to roughly mash the drained kidney beans, then stir in the tomato sauce, crushed garlic and chilli powder. Season with salt and pepper.

4 Sprinkle plenty of fine ground semolina on your wooden peel or your work surface, then place the dough rounds on top. Spread half of the tomato and bean mixture over each, using the back of a tablespoon to spread it around evenly. Leave a border round the edge of about 2.5cm/1in, so the mixture doesn't spill on to the oven floor.

5 Place half of the salami slices on to each pizza, then tear the mozzarella into small pieces and scatter over the top. Season with salt and pepper. Drizzle over a little olive oil.

6 Use the peel to place the pizzas on the base of the oven, flicking them gently to help them slide off. Putting plenty of fine ground semolina on the peel helps transfer the pizza on to the oven base; it functions like miniature ball-bearings.

7 Bake the pizzas on the oven floor for about 90 seconds, turning if necessary, until the bases are crispy and the toppings are charred and bubbling. You don't need to close the door, as the oven is very hot.

8 Use the wooden peel to take the pizzas out and put on a large wooden board. Allow to set for a minute and then use a large, sharp knife to cut them into pieces. Sprinkle with Tabasco sauce before serving.

MAKES 2 30CM/12IN PIZZAS

½ quantity pizza dough (page 24)
125g/4¼oz cooked red kidney
   beans, rinsed and well drained
60ml/4 tbsp tomato sauce (page 25)
1 clove garlic, peeled and crushed
5–10ml/1–2 tsp chilli powder
50g/2oz thinly sliced salami
50g/2oz mozzarella balls
salt and ground black pepper
olive oil, for drizzling
fine ground semolina, for sprinkling
Tabasco sauce, to serve

PER PIZZA Energy 620kcal/2064kJ; Protein 27g; Carbohydrate 70g, of which sugars 4g; Fat 29g, of which saturates 10g; Cholesterol 42mg; Calcium 258mg; Fibre 8.8g; Sodium 1908mg.

½ quantity pizza dough (page 24)
30ml/2 tbsp good-quality basil
   pesto
30ml/2 tbsp golden marjoram or
   marjoram leaves, roughly
   chopped
4 thin slices Parma ham, gently
   ripped into pieces
4 artichoke hearts in olive oil,
   drained and each cut into 4
   lengthways
50g/2oz Gruyère cheese, grated
salt and ground black pepper
olive oil, for drizzling
fine ground semolina, for sprinkling

PER PIZZA Energy 686kcal/2873kJ; Protein 32g;
Carbohydrate 58g, of which sugars 2g; Fat 38g, of
which saturates 13g; Cholesterol 41mg; Calcium
559mg; Fibre 2.8g; Sodium 2194mg.

PIZZA WITH ARTICHOKE HEARTS, PARMA HAM AND BASIL PESTO

This pizza has basil pesto as a base. You can make your own or use a good quality fresh one. The Parma ham crisps up beautifully in the wood-fired oven.

1 Build up the fire in the oven until it is about 400°C/750°F, this will take about 60 minutes. When it is up to temperature, push the fire to the back of the oven with a metal peel or coal hook, and close the oven door.

2 Divide the pizza dough into two and roll out into rounds roughly 30cm/12in wide and 3mm/⅛in thick. Put the bases on a wooden peel, or work surface, on a layer of semolina, to help prevent the dough from sticking.

3 Spread 15ml/1 tbsp of the pesto over the pizza base, using the back of a spoon to spread it around evenly. Leave a border of about 2.5cm/1in, so it doesn't spill on to the oven base during cooking.

4 Sprinkle half the marjoram over the pesto then place half the torn Parma ham, two of the artichokes, and half of the Gruyère cheese on top. Season with a little salt and black pepper, and drizzle with olive oil.

5 Use the peel to place the first pizza on the base of the oven, then sprinkle the peel again with semolina and make up the second pizza. Using plenty of semolina on the peel helps the pizzas slide off on to the oven base.

6 Bake the pizzas for about 90 seconds with the door open, until crispy and bubbling. Use a wooden peel to take the pizzas out. Allow to set for a minute, then use a large, sharp knife to cut them into pieces.

MAKES 2 30CM/12IN PIZZAS

½ quantity pizza dough (page 24)
¼ quantity caramelized roast
   shallots (page 91)
50g/2oz feta cheese, crumbled
30ml/2 tbsp fresh thyme leaves
ground black pepper
olive oil for drizzling
fine ground semolina, for sprinkling

PER PIZZA Energy 703kcal/2971kJ; Protein 26g;
Carbohydrate 118g, of which sugars 3g; Fat 18g, of
which saturates 8g; Cholesterol 35mg; Calcium
434mg; Fibre 5.8g; Sodium 2744mg.

CARAMELIZED SHALLOT AND FETA PIZZA

Italians call pizzas without a tomato base 'blonde' pizzas, and this recipe is a great way of using the caramelized roast shallots recipe – the sweet, slow-cooked onions and garlic, in their tangy balsamic sauce, go well with the salty feta and the crisp pizza bases, and the fire from the oven adds a delicious smokiness.

1 Build up the fire in the oven until it is about 400°C/750°F, this will take about 60 minutes. When it is up to temperature, push the fire to the back of the oven with a metal peel or coal hook. Close the door to keep the heat inside.

2 Divide the pizza dough in half and use a rolling pin to shape into rounds roughly 30cm/12in wide and 3mm/⅛in thick. Put a dough round on a peel, on a layer of semolina, to stop the dough from sticking.

3 Spread half of the shallot mixture over the base and sprinkle over half the feta and thyme. Drizzle with olive oil and grind over some more black pepper.

4 Use the peel to flick the first pizza on to the base of the oven. Then make the second pizza the same way. Always put plenty of semolina on the peel – this will help the pizzas slide off on to the oven base.

5 Bake the pizzas on the oven floor for about 90 seconds with the door open, until the bases are crispy and the toppings are charring and bubbling.

6 Use the wooden or metal peel to take the pizzas out of the oven and put them on a large wooden board. Allow the pizzas to set for a minute and then use a large, sharp knife to cut into pieces.

COURGETTE, CHILLI AND MINT PIZZA

Courgettes – or zucchini – cook really well on pizzas, especially if you use a potato peeler or mandolin to cut them into very thin ribbons. The intense heat from the wood-fired oven cooks them very quickly, giving them a flavourful charring, but because they have a high water content, they don't dry out.

1 Build up the fire in the oven until it is about 400°C/750°F, this will take about 60 minutes. When it is up to temperature, push the fire to the back of the oven with a metal peel or coal hook, and keep the oven door closed.

2 Slice the courgettes into thin ribbons using a mandolin or a wide potato peeler. In a large bowl toss the courgette ribbons with the red onion, chilli flakes, lemon rind and about 45ml/3 tbsp of olive oil. Season well.

3 Divide the pizza dough in half and shape into rounds roughly 30cm/12in wide and 3mm/⅛in thick. Put a base on a wooden peel on some of the fine ground semolina, so that the dough won't stick.

4 Place half of the courgette mixture on the base. Shave slivers of Parmesan on the top of the pizza, then use the peel to flick it on to the base of the oven, leaving space for the second pizza. Assemble the second pizza, putting plenty of semolina on the peel, to help it slide off on to the oven base.

5 Bake each pizza on the oven floor for about 90 seconds, until the bases are crispy and the toppings are slightly charring. You don't need to close the door, as the oven is very hot.

6 Use the wooden peel to take the pizzas out and put on a large wooden board. Sprinkle over the fresh mint and allow the pizzas to set for a minute, then cut into pieces.

MAKES 2 30CM/12IN PIZZAS

2 medium courgettes (zucchini), 1 green and 1 yellow, if possible
1 medium red onion, very finely sliced
5ml/1 tsp dried chilli flakes
rind of half a lemon, finely grated
45ml/3 tbsp olive oil
½ quantity pizza dough (page 24)
Parmesan, for shaving
30ml/2 tbsp chopped fresh mint
salt and ground black pepper
fine ground semolina, for sprinkling

PER PIZZA Energy 555kcal/2324kJ; Protein 14g; Carbohydrate 66g, of which sugars 7g; Fat 28g, of which saturates 5g; Cholesterol 5mg; Calcium 211mg; Fibre 4.0g; Sodium 1254mg.

PIZZA WITH ROASTED BUTTERNUT SQUASH, CHILLI AND MOZZARELLA

The roasted butternut squash on this pizza makes a lovely and unusual topping, and the smoky charred finish it gets in the wood-fired oven suits its earthy texture, especially when complemented by the chilli, red onion and creamy mozzarella.

1 Build up the fire in the oven until it is about 400°C/750°F, this will take about 60 minutes. When it is at temperature, push the fire to the back of the oven with a metal peel or coal hook, and close the oven door to keep the heat inside.

2 Divide the pizza dough into two and roll out into rounds roughly 30cm/12in wide and 3mm/⅛in thick. Sprinkle a wooden peel with fine ground semolina, to prevent the dough from sticking, and put a pizza base on top.

3 Spread half of the mashed squash over the base and sprinkle over half of the sliced red onion and a couple of pinches of chilli flakes.

4 Tear the mozzarella into small pieces and add half of it to the pizza. Drizzle over a little olive oil and season with salt and pepper.

5 Use the wooden peel to flick the first pizza on to the base of the oven and then assemble the second pizza.

6 Bake each pizza in the oven for about 90 seconds with the door open, until the pizzas are golden and bubbling.

7 Use the wooden peel to take the pizzas out of the oven and put on a large wooden board. Allow to stand for a minute, then cut into slices with a sharp knife.

MAKES 2 30CM/12IN PIZZAS

175g/6oz roasted butternut squash (see cook's tip below)
½ quantity pizza dough (page 24)
1 medium red onion, finely sliced
5–10ml/1–2 tsp dried red chilli flakes
90g/3½oz mozzarella, well drained
salt and ground black pepper
olive oil, for drizzling
fine ground semolina, for sprinkling

> **COOK'S TIP**
> The butternut squash can be roasted in advance when you are using the oven for something else – you don't need to heat it up especially. The mash can then be chilled or frozen. Place the squash in an ovenproof dish, prick with a sharp knife and bake until tender at about 180°C/350°F. If the oven temperature is lower, just leave it in for a little longer. When cool, skin, seed and mash the flesh with some salt and black pepper.

PER PIZZA Energy 461kcal/1946kJ; Protein 19g; Carbohydrate 71g, of which sugars 9g; Fat 13g, of which saturates 7g; Cholesterol 26mg; Calcium 26mg; Fibre 4.0g; Sodium 1396mg.

MAKES 2 30CM/12IN PIZZAS

½ quantity pizza dough (page 24)
125g/4¼oz waxy potatoes, peeled,
    parboiled, cooled and very
    thinly sliced
30ml/2 tbsp chopped thyme leaves
90g/3½oz fresh chorizo sausage,
    finely diced
50g/2oz small mozzarella balls,
    drained
salt and ground black pepper
olive oil, for drizzling
fine ground semolina, for sprinkling

PER PIZZA Energy 542kcal/2281kJ; Protein 24g;
Carbohydrate 70g, of which sugars 3g; Fat 20g, of
which saturates 9g; Cholesterol 17mg; Calcium
259mg; Fibre 3.9g; Sodium 1558mg.

VARIATION

Replace the chorizo with
sun-dried tomatoes and a
sprinkle of smoked paprika.

POTATO AND CHORIZO PIZZA

Waxy potatoes are needed for this topping, as they hold together better than floury potatoes. Using fresh chorizo works well in the recipe as the savoury oils ooze out into the potatoes and the base, adding a delicious intensity of flavour.

1 Build up the fire in the oven until it is about 400°C/750°F, this will take about 60 minutes. When it is up to temperature, push the fire to the back of the oven with a metal peel or coal hook and close the oven door.

2 Divide the pizza dough into two and roll out into rounds roughly 30cm/12in wide and 3mm/⅛in thick. Put the bases directly on to a wooden peel, on some of the fine ground semolina, as this is a difficult pizza to move once it has been assembled.

3 Arrange the sliced potatoes evenly over the pizza base, then sprinkle over half the thyme leaves, followed by half the diced chorizo.

4 Tear the little mozzarella balls in half and and place half the pieces on top of the pizza. Season well with salt and pepper and drizzle over a little olive oil.

5 Flick the first pizza on to the oven floor, then use the peel to make the second pizza in the same way.

6 Bake each pizza on the oven floor for about 90 seconds, you don't need to close the door, as the oven is very hot, and the flames help to char the topping. Use the wooden peel to take the pizzas out, and put on a large wooden board. Allow to set for a minute and then use a sharp knife to cut into slices.

PEAR, LEEK AND BLUE CHEESE PIZZA

Pears, leeks and blue cheese are a classic combination and go well together as a topping for wood-fired pizzas. A mild, soft blue cheese works well, such as Roquefort, but you can also use the harder, stronger blue cheeses, like Stilton.

MAKES 2 30CM/12IN PIZZAS

2–3 medium leeks, trimmed, washed, drained and sliced thinly
30ml/2 tbsp olive oil
25g/1oz butter
½ quantity pizza dough (page 24)
2–3 ripe pears, peeled, cored and thinly sliced from the bottom to the top (the red skinned ones look nice)
115g/4oz blue cheese (eg Roquefort, Gorgonzola, Stilton)
salt and ground black pepper
olive oil, for drizzling
fine ground semolina, for sprinkling

1 Build the fire in the oven to a temperature of around 150°C/300°F, which will take about 30 minutes. When it is at temperature, push the fire to the back of the oven with a metal peel or coal hook.

2 Put the leeks in an ovenproof dish with the olive oil and butter. Cover with a lid and put the pan in the oven, close the door and bake for 15–20 minutes, until the leeks have softened but not coloured.

3 Take the pan out of the oven, making sure you wear gauntlets or long oven gloves or use a thick oven cloth. Set aside to cool.

4 Build up the fire on the base of the oven so that the temperature reaches 400°C/750°F, which will take another 30–45 minutes. Push the fire to the back of the oven with a metal peel or coal hook.

5 Meanwhile, divide the pizza dough into two and roll out into rounds roughly 30cm/12in wide and 3mm/⅛in thick. Put the bases on a wooden peel on top of a sprinkling of fine semolina, to prevent the dough from sticking to the surface.

6 Quarter, core and thinly slice the pears from the top to the bottom. Cut the cheese into cubes.

7 Divide the softened leeks between the pizza bases, and use the back of a spoon to spread evenly over the surface. Arrange the pear slices over the top.

8 Crumble half of the blue cheese on top of each pizza. Season with salt and pepper, but don't use too much salt, as the blue cheese may already be quite salty.

9 Drizzle a little olive oil over the surface of each pizza and place them one at a time on the oven floor.

10 Bake the pizzas for about 90 seconds with the door open, until the bases are crisp, the pears are tender and the blue cheese has melted.

11 Use the wooden peel to take the pizzas out and put them on a large wooden board. Let them stand for a minute before cutting into slices with a large, sharp knife.

PER PIZZA Energy 863kcal/3689kJ; Protein 26g; Carbohydrate 81g, of which sugars 24g; Fat 53g, of which saturates 24g; Cholesterol 89mg; Calcium 356mg; Fibre 6.1g; Sodium 1780mg.

HAM AND RICOTTA CALZONE

A calzone is the Cornish pasty of the pizza world – a lovely crisp container holding a delicious moist filling. You need to roll the dough thicker than for a regular pizza, so it can hold the filling easily. Only use fillings that are already cooked for calzone.

1 Build up the fire in the oven until it is about 300°C/570°F, this will take about 50 minutes. When it is up to temperature, push the fire to the back of the oven with a metal peel or coal hook. Close the oven door to retain the heat.

2 On a surface sprinkled with plenty of ground semolina, or directly on to a wooden peel, roll out the dough to make two rounds 25cm/10in wide and 5mm/¼in thick.

3 In a large bowl, mix the ricotta with the ham, rocket, Parmesan and chilli flakes, and season well with salt and pepper.

4 Spread half the ricotta mixture over each of the bases, leaving a 2.5cm/1in margin.

5 Fold the dough over and seal the edges, making sure you get rid of any air pockets that will swell up and burst during cooking. Drizzle a little olive oil over the top.

6 Sprinkle some semolina on a wooden peel, then flick the calzones on to it and place them on the base of the oven. Put plenty of semolina on the peel, to help them slide off on to the oven base.

7 Shut the oven door and bake the calzones for 7–8 minutes, until golden brown. Use the wooden peel to take the calzones out of the oven. Put the calzones on a wooden board, let them stand for a few minutes before eating as the filling will be very hot.

MAKES 2 CALZONES

½ quantity pizza dough (page 24)
240g/8½oz ricotta
115g/4oz cooked ham, finely sliced
3 handfuls fresh rocket (arugula)
90g/3½oz freshly grated Parmesan
  or pecorino cheese
2.5ml/½ tsp chilli flakes
salt and ground black pepper
olive oil, for drizzling
fine ground semolina, for sprinkling

PER CALZONE Energy 762kcal/3282kJ; Protein 53g; Carbohydrate 61g, of which sugars 4g; Fat 53g, of which saturates 24g; Cholesterol 89mg; Calcium 865mg; Fibre 3.2g; Sodium 2874mg.

MIDDLE EASTERN SPICED LAMB PIZZA

This pizza, topped with spicy lamb, gets a delicious charring in the wood-fired oven. The base gets wonderfully crispy, and the melted feta cheese adds a hint of saltiness. A perfect pizza for a long summer evening as the sun goes down.

1 Build up the fire in the oven until it is about 350°C/660°F, this will take about 60 minutes. When it is up to temperature, push the fire to the back of the oven with a metal peel or coal hook and close the oven door.

2 In a large bowl use a wooden spoon or a fork to break up the minced lamb, then mix in the chopped onion, garlic, chilli, tomato sauce and red wine vinegar. Season well with salt and black pepper.

3 Divide the pizza dough into two and on a flat surface roll out into rounds roughly 30cm/12in wide and 3mm/⅛in thick. Put a base on a wooden peel on some of the fine ground semolina, to help prevent the dough from sticking to the surface.

4 Top the base with half the lamb mixture and sprinkle half of the feta cheese over the top. Drizzle over some olive oil.

5 Use the peel to flick the first pizza on on to the base of the oven, leaving space for the second one. Assemble the second pizza the same way.

6 Bake the pizzas on the oven floor for about 3 minutes, until the bases are crispy and the toppings are charred and bubbling. Use the wooden peel to take them out and put on a large wooden board.

7 Allow to set for a minute, sprinkle over the fresh mint leaves and then use a large, sharp knife to cut them into pieces.

MAKES 2 30cm/12in PIZZAS

½ quantity pizza dough (page 24)
115g/4oz minced (ground) lamb
1 medium onion, very finely
 chopped
2 cloves garlic, peeled and crushed
1 fresh red chilli, seeded and very
 finely chopped
60ml/4 tbsp tomato sauce (page 25)
15ml/1 tbsp red wine vinegar
50g/2oz feta cheese, crumbled
30ml/2 tbsp olive oil
30ml/2 tbsp fresh chopped mint
 leaves
salt and ground black pepper
fine ground semolina, for sprinkling

PER PIZZA Energy 670kcal/2804kJ; Protein 27g; Carbohydrate 67g, of which sugars 8g; Fat 34g, of which saturates 11g; Cholesterol 66mg; Calcium 257mg; Fibre 4.6g; Sodium 1724mg.

FISH AND SEAFOOD

Cooking any kind of seafood in the wood-fired oven is a perfect way of keeping it deliciously moist – it's definitely the best way we've found of cooking fish. The high temperatures seem to steam the fish from the inside and char it on the outside so you get a great combination of flavours. You can also use the lower temperatures of a falling oven to great effect in a more slowly cooked dish like a soup, where the fish is gently poached in a tomato base – equally fantastic.

SALMON WITH BAKED NEW POTATOES

Salmon is a robust fish that absorbs strong flavours well – here it has a topping of fresh lime, chilli, zesty ginger and sweet honey. Baking salmon in a hot oven makes it cook very quickly, giving it a good golden-brown crust.

SERVES 6

6 pieces of salmon fillet, about
    175g/6oz each, scaled but with
    the skin still on
30ml/2 tbsp runny honey
juice and grated rind of 1 lime
2.5cm/1in cube fresh root ginger,
    peeled and grated
1 small fresh red chilli, seeded, and
    very finely chopped
1kg/2¼lb mini new potatoes,
    washed but not peeled
60ml/4 tbsp olive oil
salt and ground black pepper

Energy 546kcal/2284kJ; Protein 39g; Carbohydrate
31g, of which sugars 6g; Fat 30g, of which saturates
5g; Cholesterol 90mg; Calcium 49mg; Fibre 2.2g;
Sodium 167mg.

1 Build up the fire in the oven until the temperature reaches 200°C/400°F, this will take about 50 minutes. When it is up to temperature, push the fire to the back of the oven with a metal peel or coal hook, and close the door to keep the heat inside.

2 Line a baking tray or ovenproof dish with baking parchment and put the salmon fillets on the top.

3 Mix together the honey, lime juice and rind, ginger and fresh chilli. Season well with salt and pepper. Spread the honey mixture over the top of each piece of salmon. Leave to marinate for 20 minutes.

4 Toss the potatoes with the oil and season well. Place in a roasting pan in a single layer.

5 Place the roasting pan of potatoes on the oven floor, manoeuvring it around as needed with a metal peel.

6 Close the door and bake for 20 minutes. After 20 minutes, open the door and place the baking sheet of salmon in the oven for 8–10 minutes (depending on the thickness of the fish), until the salmon is cooked and golden brown but still moist inside. The potatoes should be tender as well.

7 Take the fish and the potatoes out of the oven, using a metal peel to bring the trays to the door. Place a piece of salmon on each of six warmed plates and pour over any juices from the baking tray. Serve at once with a fresh green herb salad and some of the roasted new potatoes.

BREAM BAKED IN SALT

Baking fish covered in salt in the wood-fired oven is a technique that has been used for hundreds of years – the heat makes the salt crust very hard, which makes it easy to remove and keeps the fish moist and tender.

1 Build up the fire on the base of the oven until the temperature reaches 240°C/475°F. This will take about 50 minutes. When it is up to temperature, push the fire to the back of the oven with a metal peel or coal hook. Close the door to keep the heat inside.

2 Wash the bream under the cold tap. Stuff the belly cavity with the lemon slices, bay leaves and fennel.

3 Put a 2.5cm/1in layer of salt on the bottom of a roasting pan large enough for the fish. Put the fish on top and cover it with another thick layer of salt, smoothing it evenly.

4 Sprinkle a little water over the top of the salt to help it form a crust. Place the roasting pan on the oven floor. Close the door and bake the fish in the oven for 30 minutes.

5 Take the pan out of the oven. Break open the salt crust and lift it off in pieces, peeling away the skin from the fish as well as all the salt. Be very careful not to drop any of the salt on to the cooked fish.

6 Fillet the fish from the bones in large pieces, transferring them to a serving plate. Serve with some lemon wedges and a green vegetable, such as wilted leeks.

SERVES 2

2 x 450g/1lb gilthead or black
   bream, cleaned, with any sharp
   fins removed
½ lemon, sliced thinly
bay leaves
fennel sprigs
1–2kg/2¼–4½lb coarse salt
wilted leeks, to serve

Energy 360kcal/1519kJ; Protein 66g; Carbohydrate 0g, of which sugars 0g; Fat 11g, of which saturates 0g; Cholesterol 143mg; Calcium 150mg; Fibre 0.0g; Sodium 1359mg.

RED MULLET IN SAGE AND PARMA HAM

This lovely fish was highly prized by the Romans, who would pay up to the equivalent of £1000 per fish for a banquet, and the saltiness of Italian Parma ham complements it really well. Baking the red mullet in a high heat turns the skin a beautiful intense pink. Use red snapper if you can't find red mullet.

1 Build up the fire on the base of the oven until the temperature reaches 240°C/475°F, this will take about 50 minutes. When it is up to temperature, push the fire to the back of the oven with a metal peel or coal hook, and close the door to keep the heat inside.

2 Lay the slices of Parma ham individually on a flat surface and put a red mullet fillet on top of each one with the flesh side facing upwards. Divide the butter over each of the fillets and sprinkle the sage over the top.

3 Wrap each fillet securely (but not too tightly) in the Parma ham and, if necessary, secure with a cocktail stick (toothpick).

4 Put the wrapped fillets in a roasting pan, with the cocktail sticks facing downwards, drizzle with a little olive oil and season well with salt and pepper.

5 Place the roasting pan on the oven floor. Bake the fish in the oven for 5–8 minutes, until the ham is crispy, the fish is cooked and the skin has become a rich pink.

6 Use the metal peel to bring the pan to the front of the oven, so you can take it out. Serve the parcels immediately, with any juices from the roasting pan poured over them and a wedge of lemon to squeeze over the top, together with warm ciabatta and rocket salad.

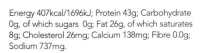

SERVES 4

4 large slices Parma ham
4 large scaled red mullet, or red snapper fillets, 225g/8oz each
50g/2oz butter
8 fresh sage leaves, chopped
salt and ground black pepper
olive oil, for drizzling
lemon wedges, warm ciabatta and rocket (arugula) salad, to serve

Energy 407kcal/1696kJ; Protein 43g; Carbohydrate 0g, of which sugars 0g; Fat 26g, of which saturates 8g; Cholesterol 26mg; Calcium 138mg; Fibre 0.0g; Sodium 737mg.

1 x 2kg/4½lb whole sea bass,
  cleaned and descaled
1 lemon, thinly sliced
3 sprigs fresh rosemary
3 fresh bay leaves
2 garlic cloves, peeled and quartered
4 spring onions (scallions), chopped
45ml/3 tbsp olive oil
salt and ground black pepper

Energy 487kcal/2039kJ; Protein 73g; Carbohydrate
2g, of which sugars 2g; Fat 21g, of which saturates
3g; Cholesterol 300mg; Calcium 520mg; Fibre 0.6g;
Sodium 360mg.

SEA BASS BAKED IN A PARCEL WITH LEMON AND HERBS

This is a simple way of cooking fish in the wood-fired oven, keeping a whole fish moist in a foil parcel. Use smaller fish for individual parcels, one for each guest if you wish, so that everyone opens them together and inhales the delicious cooking aromas as they waft out. You can also use salmon or red mullet for this recipe.

1 Build up the fire in the oven until the temperature reaches 240°C/475°F. This will take about 50 minutes. When it is up to temperature, push the fire to the back of the oven with a metal peel or coal hook. Close the door to keep the heat inside.

2 Cut two large pieces of foil, each about 60 x 60cm/24 x 24in, and put them on top of each other. Put the fish in the middle of the sheets of foil and put the lemon, rosemary, bay leaves, garlic and spring onions inside and around the fish.

3 Turn up the ends of the foil and pour the oil over the fish. Season with salt and pepper.

4 Crimp the foil edges together to make a parcel, leaving space for some air around the fish – a bit like a Cornish pasty.

5 Place the parcel on the floor of the oven, using a metal peel to do so. Close the door and bake the sea bass in the oven for 30 minutes. Open the door, carefully take out the foil parcel, using oven gloves or a metal peel to do so, and place it on a serving plate.

6 Take the parcel to the table and open it in front of your guests so they all enjoy the aroma. Carefully lift fillets of fish from the bone, and serve with some of the filling and some fresh bread.

SERVES 6 AS AN APPETIZER

12 large cleaned scallops with their
    shells, also cleaned
juice and grated rind of 1 lemon
15ml/1 tbsp chilli oil
30ml/2 tbsp olive oil
25g/1oz butter, softened
1 clove garlic, peeled and crushed
30ml/2 tbsp finely chopped fresh
    parsley
30ml/2 tbsp dried white
    breadcrumbs
salt and ground black pepper
60ml/4 tbsp roughly chopped fresh
    mint
fresh, crusty bread, to serve

Energy 293kcal/1227kJ; Protein 28g; Carbohydrate
7g, of which sugars 0g; Fat 17g, of which saturates
5g; Cholesterol 67mg; Calcium 50mg; Fibre 0.3g;
Sodium 366mg.

SCALLOPS WITH CHILLI AND MINT

Like all fish, scallops respond well to the hot temperatures in the wood-fired oven –
they get a good charring on the outside, which adds to the flavours of the recipe.
By baking the scallops in their round shells you won't have any dishes to wash.

1 Build up the fire in the oven until the temperature reaches 300°C/570°F. This will take about 60 minutes. When it is up to temperature, push the fire to the back of the oven with a metal peel or coal hook, and keep the door open to encourage a hot fire with high flames.

2 In a bowl, mix the lemon juice and grated rind with the chilli oil and olive oil, the butter, garlic, parsley and breadcrumbs. Season well.

3 Cut the scallops in half to make discs and put them with their roes back in the cleaned half shells. Divide the breadcrumb mixture over the scallops.

4 Put the shells on a baking sheet; use two if you need to. Place the baking sheets in the oven, as close to the fire as possible. Keep the door open and bake for just 4–5 minutes, until the tops are golden and sizzling.

5 Carefully move the baking sheets to the front of the oven, using a metal peel to do so. Pick up the baking sheets, but be careful to keep them level so you don't lose any of the delicious juices.

6 Sprinkle the chopped mint over the scallops and serve immediately with some fresh, crusty bread to mop up all the juices, remembering that the shells will be very hot.

MARINATED SQUID WITH HOME-MADE CHILLI MAYONNAISE

This squid, in its punchy marinade, is deliciously tender with a slight charring. This is a great recipe to use as an appetizer before using the oven to rustle up some pizzas or searing some steaks, so you're not firing up the oven for a 40-second cook-off.

1 Build up the fire on the base of the oven until the temperature reaches 300°C/570°F. This will take about 60 minutes. When it is up to temperature, push the fire to the back of the oven with a metal peel or coal hook, and close the door to maintain the temperature.

2 Slice the hood of the squid open so it is one big flat piece of flesh. Lightly score the skin into tiny diamond shapes with a sharp knife. Slice the squid and its tentacles into small bitesize pieces.

3 In a large bowl, mix together the olive oil, garlic, oregano and lemon rind. Add the squid and toss. Season well and leave to marinate for 30 minutes in the refrigerator.

4 Make the mayonnaise; put the egg yolk in a large bowl with the mustard, lemon juice and chilli powder. Season well.

5 With a balloon whisk, mix all the ingredients together thoroughly, then gradually add the sunflower oil a few drops at a time, whisking vigorously. When the mayonnaise is thick, check for seasoning and keep in the refrigerator until needed.

6 Put the marinated squid in a roasting pan in one layer (use two pans if necessary), and carefully place the roasting pans on the oven floor. Close the door and bake in the very hot oven for just 40 seconds.

7 Open the oven door and take the roasting pans out of the oven, using a metal peel to manoeuvre them to the front of the oven.

8 Quickly transfer the squid and any juices from the pans on to a serving platter and serve at once with the chilli mayonnaise and some lemon wedges and focaccia.

SERVES 6 AS AN APPETIZER

600g/1lb 6oz fresh squid, cleaned
   weight
60ml/4 tbsp olive oil
2 cloves garlic, peeled and crushed
30ml/2 tbsp fresh oregano or
   marjoram leaves, roughly
   chopped
rind of 1 lemon, very finely grated,
salt and ground black pepper
lemon wedges and focaccia,
   to serve

FOR THE CHILLI MAYONNAISE
1 egg yolk
5ml/1 tsp mustard
juice of 1 lemon
2.5–5ml/½–1 tsp chilli powder
150ml/¼ pint/⅔ cup sunflower oil

Energy 614kcal/2541kJ; Protein 24g; Carbohydrate 2g, of which sugars 0g; Fat 57g, of which saturates 8g; Cholesterol 388mg; Calcium 32mg; Fibre 0.0g; Sodium 327mg.

MEAT

Good meat cooked quickly in the searing heat of the wood-fired oven is one of life's greatest pleasures – the result is fantastically juicy meat with a delicious chargrilling from the flames. However, slow-cooked meat dishes are equally perfect for cooking in a falling oven, and it means you can use the time they are gently simmerng in the oven to go off and do other things, before coming back to enjoy a dinner that is meltingly tender and full of flavour.

JERK CHICKEN

This is a classic barbecue rub found on street food throughout the West Indies. Baking the chicken in the wood-fired oven instead of on the barbecue gives more of a surrounding heat, which cooks the meat right through. Jerk chicken is great finger food, eaten piping hot from the bone, or shredded and stuffed in a pitta with salad.

1 Put all the rub ingredients in a bowl, and mix together with a balloon whisk.

2 Put the chicken thighs into an ovenproof dish. Rub the paste into the chicken joints very well. Cover the dish with clear film (plastic wrap) and put in the refrigerator for as long as possible, preferably overnight.

3 An hour before you're ready to cook, start the fire in the oven. Build up the fire on the base of the oven until the temperature reaches 220°C/425°F. This will take about 60 minutes. Push the fire to the back of the oven with a metal peel or coal hook, and close the door to maintain the temperature.

4 Remove the clear film from the chicken and place the dish on the oven floor. Close the door and bake the chicken for 15–20 minutes, depending on the size of the joints, until cooked through. Take the dish out of the oven and insert a skewer into the thighs – if there is any pink in the juices put the dish back in the oven for another 5 minutes.

5 Squeeze some lime juice over the chicken pieces, sprinkle with the fresh coriander, then serve as they are, still piping hot. Alternatively, shred the meat from the bones first, then toss in some lime juice and coriander, and serve stuffed into warmed pitta breads with salad leaves.

SERVES 6

12 free-range chicken thighs, skinned
coriander (cilantro), chopped, and lime wedges, to serve

FOR THE JERK RUB
5ml/1 tsp each salt and ground black pepper
2.5ml/½ tsp freshly grated nutmeg
5ml/1 tsp ground cinnamon
1 medium onion, very finely chopped
15ml/1 tbsp fresh thyme leaves
2 red chillies, very finely chopped
15ml/1 tbsp demerara (raw) sugar
45ml/3 tbsp sunflower oil
juice and grated rind of 1½ limes

Energy 252kcal/1050kJ; Protein 20g; Carbohydrate 10g, of which sugars 10g; Fat 15g, of which saturates 4g; Cholesterol 108mg; Calcium 48mg; Fibre 0.4g; Sodium 394mg.

200ml/7fl oz/scant 1 cup natural (plain) yogurt
juice and grated rind of 1 lemon
1 onion, roughly chopped
2 cloves garlic, peeled
2.5cm/1in cube fresh root ginger, peeled and roughly chopped
1 small fresh red chilli, roughly chopped
5ml/1 tsp garam masala or medium curry powder
5ml/1 tsp ground coriander
5ml/1 tsp ground turmeric
2.5ml/½ tsp ground cinnamon
12 free-range chicken thighs, skinned
30ml/2 tbsp chopped fresh mint
2 limes, cut into wedges
salt and ground black pepper
naan bread and mint and cucumber raita, to serve

Energy 268kcal/1114kJ; Protein 22g; Carbohydrate 4g, of which sugars 3g; Fat 18g, of which saturates 6g; Cholesterol 114mg; Calcium 79mg; Fibre 0.4g; Sodium 154mg.

TANDOORI CHICKEN WITH RAITA

Indian spices work well in a wood-fired oven and a yogurt marinade keeps meat wonderfully juicy. Serve the chicken with naan bread and a mint and cucumber raita.

1 Put the yogurt, lemon juice and rind, onion, garlic, ginger, chilli, and ground spices into a bowl and mix with a hand blender. You can use a balloon whisk instead, but you will need to finely chop the onion, ginger, garlic and chilli first. Season well with salt and pepper.

2 Put the chicken thighs into a ceramic dish and spread the paste over. Cover with clear film (plastic wrap) and leave in the refrigerator to marinate for at least 2 hours, turning the pieces in the marinade at least once.

3 An hour before you're ready to cook, start the fire in the oven. Build up the fire until the temperature reaches 220°C/425°F, this will take about 60 minutes. Push the fire to the back of the oven with a metal peel or coal hook. Close the door to keep the heat inside.

4 Put the marinated chicken on to a wire rack over a roasting pan and daub any marinade that has come off the joints back on top.

5 Put the roasting pan and wire rack on the oven floor, and close the door. Bake the chicken for 15–20 minutes, depending on the size of the thighs, until cooked through. To test, take the pan out of the oven and insert a skewer into the centre of the largest piece – the juices will run clear if the chicken is cooked. If there is any pink in the juices put the dish back in the oven until they run clear when you retest them.

6 Serve the chicken with the mint sprinkled over the top and the lime wedges on the side to squeeze over. Eat at once with naan bread and a mint and cucumber raita.

MINT AND CUCUMBER RAITA

Peel and dice a 20cm/8in cucumber. Mix with 30ml/2 tbsp chopped fresh mint and 350g/12oz yogurt. Season and serve straightaway, or chill for up to an hour.

1 large free-range chicken, about
   2.5kg/5½lb
1 lemon
1 handful of fresh thyme
60ml/4 tbsp olive oil
200ml/7fl oz/scant 1 cup dry
   white wine
salt and ground black pepper

FOR THE WILTED GREENS
2 heads greens, such as cavolo
   nero, curly kale or spring greens
1 medium leek, washed and finely
   sliced
2 fresh red chillies, seeded, and
   very finely chopped

Energy 464kcal/1930kJ; Protein 47g; Carbohydrate
3g, of which sugars 3g; Fat 29g, of which saturates
7g; Cholesterol 183mg; Calcium 199mg; Fibre 5.6g;
Sodium 215mg.

LEMON AND THYME ROASTED CHICKEN WITH WILTED GREENS

Roast chicken is an all-time classic and surely everyone's favourite. The meat stays beautifully succulent when cooked in the wood-fired oven, while the skin becomes golden and crisp with a hint of smokiness. Don't throw the carcass away after your meal – use it to make the best-ever chicken stock in your falling oven.

1 Build up the fire in the oven until the temperature reaches 190°C/375°F. This will take about 45 minutes. Push the fire to the back of the oven with a metal peel or coal hook.

2 Cut the lemon into quarters and push into the chicken cavity, along with the handful of fresh thyme. Rub 30ml/2 tbsp of the olive oil over the chicken and season well with salt and pepper. Place the chicken in a roasting pan and pour the wine into the base. Cover with foil and bake in the oven with the door closed for 20 minutes per 500g/1¼lb plus an extra 20 minutes.

3 Open the door 30 minutes before the end of cooking, and take the roasting pan out of the oven. Take the foil off the chicken then return to the oven to let the chicken skin turn crispy and golden brown.

4 Test if the chicken is cooked by inserting a skewer into the thigh – if the juices run clear it is done. Take the bird out of the oven and leave it to rest in a warm place for 20 minutes.

5 While the chicken is resting, finely chop the greens and toss with the leek, red chillies and the rest of the olive oil. Season well with salt and pepper. Put in an ovenproof pan and cover. Bake in the oven with the door closed for 10–12 minutes, until the greens are cooked through and tender.

6 Slice or joint the chicken and serve it with the juices from the roasting pan and the greens and leeks.

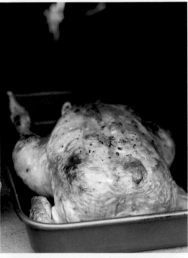

WOOD-FIRED OVEN CHICKEN STOCK

Make stock with the chicken carcass by putting it into an ovenproof pan with a carrot, an onion, a stick of celery, parsley stalks, thyme leaves, a bay leaf and 10 black peppercorns. Add enough water to just cover, put a lid on the pan and put it in the wood-fired oven with the door closed. The temperature will be falling but that's fine – you want a low heat. Leave it in there all night, and in the morning strain the stock; use as a base for sauces, soups and casseroles. A stock made this way is full of flavour, with a hint of smokiness.

CHILLI CON CARNE

Slow cooking is a great way to use the wood-fired oven – it really lets the flavours of the dish come into their own, especially in recipes like this one, where the spices can mellow and soften over a long period. Chilli is even better if you can make it in advance and then reheat it, so if you've fired up your oven for a pizza party, put this in when you've finished and leave to cook in the falling oven for the next day.

SERVES 6

1kg/2¼lb lean good-quality minced (ground) beef
60ml/4 tbsp sunflower oil
2 onions, chopped
2 cloves garlic, peeled and crushed
2 red (bell) peppers, seeded and thinly sliced
1 fresh green chilli, seeded and very finely chopped
15ml/1 tbsp chilli powder, or less if you don't want too much heat
5ml/1 tsp ground cinnamon
5ml/1 tsp smoked paprika
5ml/1 tsp unsweetened cocoa powder
1 quantity tomato sauce (page 25)
15ml/1 tbsp sundried tomato purée (paste)
15ml/1 tbsp fresh thyme leaves
chicken or beef stock
6 medium potatoes, washed and pricked
1 x 450g can kidney beans, drained and rinsed
salt and ground black pepper
sour cream, grated Cheddar cheese and tomato salad, to serve

Energy 612kcal/2562kJ; Protein 46g; Carbohydrate 43g, of which sugars 12g; Fat 30g, of which saturates 9g; Cholesterol 93mg; Calcium 99mg; Fibre 9.3g; Sodium 425mg.

1 Build up the fire in the oven until the temperature reaches 230°C/450°F, this will take about 45 minutes. When it is up to temperature, push the fire to the back of the oven with a metal peel or coal hook.

2 In about three or four batches (otherwise the meat will just stew and not fry) put the minced beef in a large ovenproof dish and bake in the oven, with the door open, for about 5 minutes or until dark brown. Take the pan out of the oven and use the back of a fork to bash the lumps into fine granules of meat. Put the cooked mince into a large bowl and repeat with the next batch until it is all cooked.

3 Leave the oven door open to allow the temperature to fall to about 180°C/350°F.

4 In the same ovenproof dish as you cooked the beef in, add the sunflower oil, onions, garlic, red peppers and fresh chilli. Mix together, put a lid on the dish and put on the oven floor, door closed, for 10 minutes, until the onions and peppers have softened.

5 Take the dish out of the oven and stir in the chilli powder, cinnamon, smoked paprika and cocoa, put the lid back on the dish, put the dish back in the oven, close the door and cook for another minute to get the raw flavour out of the spices.

6 Take the dish out of the oven and stir in the cooked beef, then add the tomato sauce, tomato purée and thyme leaves. Add enough stock so that the liquid is about 2.5cm/1in above the level of the meat. Season well with salt and pepper and mix together.

7 Place the dish in the oven once more, and at this stage add the prepared potatoes on the floor of the oven, arranged around the dish, close the door and leave undisturbed for 1½–2 hours.

8 Take the dish out of the oven 20 minutes before the end of cooking. Stir in the kidney beans and put back in the oven with the lid on and the door closed, so that the beans heat through.

9 Serve with the potatoes, topped with grated cheese and sour cream, and accompanied by tomato salad.

VARIATION

Instead of baked potatoes you could serve the chilli with tortilla chips, quickly warmed in the oven, with grated cheese on top. The chilli is also delicious with basmati rice or in floury tortillas with some crunchy green salad.

45ml/3 tbsp olive oil

30ml/2 tbsp chopped fresh oregano
or marjoram

30ml/2 tbsp fresh thyme, chopped

1 leg of lamb – about 2.5kg/5½lb

1 whole bulb of garlic, unpeeled
and sliced in two through the
equator

600g/1lb 6oz small waxy potatoes,
washed

2 lemons, quartered

3 fresh bay leaves

200ml/7fl oz/scant 1 cup dry
white wine

salt and ground black pepper

bread, and spinach salad, to serve

Energy 400kcal/1671kJ; Protein 36g; Carbohydrate
17g, of which sugars 2g; Fat 21g, of which saturates
7g; Cholesterol 123mg; Calcium 37mg; Fibre 1.3g;
Sodium 194mg.

KLEFTICO

This delicious Greek recipe for slow-cooked leg of lamb with potatoes, lemon and oregano is named after the klefts, bandits who lived in the Greek mountains during the Ottoman Empire. The klefts would steal goats and sheep from neighbouring villages and cook them in sealed pots in a pit in the ground, so that the smoke from a fire wouldn't be seen. You don't need to go to such an extreme, however, as this recipe is a perfect dish for the wood-fired oven; the gentle heat of the falling oven keeps the meat moist and fragrant. Once the lamb is in the oven you are free to simply let it cook, with no further interference, until you are ready to eat. Serve the lamb and potatoes with bread and a lemon-dressed spinach salad.

1 Build up the fire in the oven until the temperature reaches 180°C/350°F. This will take about 40 minutes. When it is up to temperature, push the fire to the back of the oven with a metal peel or coal hook. Keep the door closed to keep the heat inside.

2 In a small bowl, mix together the oil, oregano and thyme and then use your hands to rub it all over the lamb. Place the lamb in a large ovenproof dish that has a close fitting lid.

3 Place the halved garlic bulb, potatoes, lemon quarters and bay leaves around the lamb, then pour the wine in to the bottom of the dish. Season well with salt and pepper.

4 Put some foil over the dish and place the lid on top – this gives a very tight seal around the lid, which will keep the meat moist.

5 Place the ovenproof dish on the oven floor. Close the door and leave the lamb to cook for 3–4 hours, until it is meltingly tender and falling off the bone; the potatoes will now be completely tender.

6 Don't worry about the temperature in the oven gradually dropping as the lamb is cooking; if you leave it for another hour it won't spoil.

7 Once the lamb is cooked, take the ovenproof dish out of the oven. Serve the meat in chunks pulled from the bone, it will be too tender to slice, with some good bread and a salad of baby spinach and fresh herbs.

> **COOK'S TIP**
>
> Shoulder of lamb is very good in this dish, as well as leg, but trim off any excess fat before cooking. If you can get mutton then that is even better as it has loads of flavour and responds really well to the slow cooking in a covered dish.

LAMB AND PRUNE TAGINE WITH MOROCCAN SPICES

This is a lovely slow-cooked one-pot dish that you can put in the falling wood-fired oven and come back to hours later for a perfectly cooked meal. The gently braised lamb is delicious and the prunes, which become meltingly tender, create a luscious, dark, sweet gravy that you can mop up with flatbreads or couscous. Tagines are traditionally cooked in the conical dishes of the same name, which allow the moisture to stay in the dish while it is cooking, but if you don't have one an ovenproof dish works just fine. This recipe is also very good made with mutton or even goat. You can get pomegranate molasses from Middle Eastern stores.

1 Build up the fire in the oven until the temperature reaches 150°C/300°F. This will take about 30 minutes. When it is up to temperature, push the fire to the back of the oven with a metal peel or coal hook. Keep the door closed to retain the heat inside. If you have already cooked something at a high temperature – maybe some flat bread – then this is the ideal dish to put in the oven to utilize the falling temperature.

2 Trim the lamb of any sinew, and cut into 2.5cm/1in cubes. Place the lamb in a large bowl and mix in the onions, garlic, spices, prunes and pomegranate molasses. Season well with salt and pepper.

3 Put the lamb mixture into a tagine, or large ovenproof dish and stir in enough chicken stock to just about cover the lamb. Seal the dish with a tight-fitting lid.

4 Place the tagine or ovenproof dish on the oven floor. Close the oven door and bake in the oven for around 2–3 hours, until the meat is tender and the stock and prunes have made a rich, dark sauce.

5 The temperature will be quite low now, so if you want to keep the tagine in there to keep warm that's fine; it shouldn't spoil. If you feel the meat is drying out a little, just stir in a bit more stock.

6 When you are ready, take out the ovenproof dish. Sprinkle the fresh mint over the meat and serve with couscous and a tomato and onion salad.

> **COOK'S TIP**
> Long slow cooking make the cheaper cuts of meat become melting and tender. Like most slow-cooked dishes if you can make it in advance and reheat it the next day, the flavours have a chance to become even more delicious.

> **VARIATION**
> Beef in place of the lamb, and apricots instead of prunes make a succulent alternative.

SERVES 4

1kg/2¼lb shoulder of lamb, boned
2 red onions, sliced
2 cloves garlic, peeled and crushed
1 fresh red chilli, seeded and finely
  chopped
15ml/1 tbsp ground coriander
5ml/1 tsp ground cumin
1 stick of cinnamon
200g/7oz pitted prunes, roughly
  chopped
30ml/2 tbsp pomegranate molasses
600ml/1 pint/2½ cups – 900ml/
  1½ pints/3¾ cups chicken stock,
  depending on the size and shape
  of your ovenproof dish
45ml/3 tbsp chopped fresh mint
salt and ground black pepper
couscous and a tomato and red
  onion salad, to serve

Energy 482kcal/2022kJ; Protein 45g; Carbohydrate 30g, of which sugars 27g; Fat 21g, of which saturates 9g; Cholesterol 150mg; Calcium 92mg; Fibre 7.5g; Sodium 411mg.

LAMB KOFTAS WITH TOMATO SALSA

This is a great recipe to cook with children, especially if they've helped to make the pittas to serve with them. Making the koftas is easy, and the high heat in the oven cooks the lamb so quickly, there's no time for anyone to lose interest and wander away. You can also make the koftas with minced beef or chicken.

1 Put the minced lamb in a large bowl and add the pistachios, herbs, cumin, coriander, cinnamon and plenty of salt and pepper. Use clean hands to squidge everything together and mix the ingredients well.

2 Take a spoonful of the mixture and, with wet hands (this helps to keep the koftas smooth), roll into balls about the size of a whole walnut. Flatten slightly and put on a plate. Chill for 60 minutes.

3 Build up the fire in the oven until the temperature reaches 250°C/480°F, this will take about 60 minutes. When it is up to temperature, push the fire to the back of the oven with a metal peel or coal hook, and close the door to maintain the temperature.

4 Make the salsa by mixing together both kinds of tomatoes with the red onion, garlic, fresh chilli, mint, and lime juice and rind in a large bowl. Season with salt and pepper and leave to stand for a few minutes before transferring to a serving dish.

5 Skewer the koftas on to 12 flat metal skewers and lie them on a roasting pan. Place on the oven floor, close the door and bake for 4–5 minutes, until cooked through.

6 Take the baking tray of koftas out of the oven. Place the pitta breads on the oven floor for a couple of seconds to warm through.

7 Serve the koftas with the tomato salsa, hummus and warmed pitta breads.

SERVES 6

1kg/2¼lb minced (ground) lamb
100g/3¾oz pistachios, shelled and
 finely chopped
30ml/2 tbsp chopped fresh mint
30ml/2 tbsp chopped fresh
 coriander (cilantro)
30ml/2 tsp ground cumin
30ml/2 tsp ground coriander
15ml/1 tsp ground cinnamon
salt and ground black pepper
hummus and pitta breads, to serve

FOR THE TOMATO SALSA
4 large ripe tomatoes, skinned,
 seeded and roughly chopped
100g/3¾oz cherry tomatoes,
 quartered
1 small red onion, very finely
 chopped
1 clove garlic, peeled and crushed
1 fresh red chilli, seeded and very
 finely chopped
30ml/2 tbsp chopped fresh mint
juice and grated rind of 1 lime

Energy 386kcal/1612kJ; Protein 38g; Carbohydrate 7g, of which sugars 6g; Fat 23g, of which saturates 7g; Cholesterol 123mg; Calcium 88mg; Fibre 1.9g; Sodium 285mg.

1kg/2¼lb shoulder of pork, boned
   with the skin scored
45ml/3 tbsp olive oil
2 cloves garlic, peeled and crushed
15ml/1 tbsp each of chopped fresh
   sage, thyme and rosemary
salt and ground black pepper
white beans with sage and garlic
   (page 86), to serve

> **COOK'S TIP**
> ....
> This slow-roasted pork is ideal
> for a falling oven that was fired
> up for pizzas or seared steaks.

Energy 600kcal/2494kJ; Protein 39g; Carbohydrate
1g, of which sugars 0g; Fat 49g, of which saturates
15g; Cholesterol 120mg; Calcium 49mg; Fibre 0.0g;
Sodium 209mg.

PORCHETTA

This classic Italian recipe would once have been cooked in the communal clay ovens of villages all over Italy. Pork shoulder is a sadly overlooked piece of meat, but with its generous layer of fat on top it responds really well to slow roasting. If there are any leftovers the next day, it is delicious shredded with gherkins in a sandwich.

1 Build up the fire on the base of the oven until the temperature reaches 150°C/300°F. This will take about 30 minutes. When it is up to temperature, push the fire to the back of the oven with a metal peel or coal hook, and close the door.

2 In a small bowl, mix the oil, crushed garlic and chopped herbs together and season well with salt and pepper.

3 Rub the herb mix right into the flesh of the pork and roll up the piece of meat, tying to secure it with a piece of string. Put it in a roasting pan, skin side up.

4 Place the roasting pan on the oven floor and close the door.

5 Bake the meat in the oven for about 2 hours, until the meat is completely tender and falling apart and the skin is golden and crunchy. Don't baste the pork during cooking, otherwise the skin will become soggy.

6 Serve the porchetta hot, cut into chunks with white beans with sage and garlic (page 86), which can be cooked in the oven at the same time as the pork. Porchetta is also delicious served with braised potatoes and a rocket (arugula) salad.

RABBIT STEW WITH APRICOTS AND WHITE WINE

Rabbit is a delicious and inexpensive meat that seems to have fallen out of favour, although it is full of flavour and low in fat. It can be purchased from butchers or local farmers' markets, both of which will do all the skinning and jointing for you. This is another recipe that works well in a falling wood-fired oven, as the gentle heat keeps the rabbit moist and succulent. Serve with baked sweet potatoes.

1 Build up the fire on the base of the oven until the temperature reaches 180°C/350°F, this will take about 40 minutes. When it is up to temperature, push the fire to the back of the oven with a metal peel or coal hook. Close the door to keep the heat inside.

2 Put the butter and the oil in a large ovenproof dish with the onion, carrot and bacon lardons. Cover, and place in the oven, door closed, for 10 minutes.

3 When the vegetables have softened, remove the lid, stir in the flour and season.

4 Gradually stir the wine and chicken stock into the vegetables until smooth then add the rabbit, apricots and rosemary. Stir again and put the lid back on the dish.

5 Place the ovenproof dish back on the oven floor. Close the door and bake the stew in the oven for around 1½ hours.

6 When the rabbit is cooked, sprinkle over the parsley and serve with baked sweet potatoes – which you can put in the oven to bake alongside the rabbit. Braised red cabbage is another good accompaniment.

SERVES 6–8

50g/2oz butter
30ml/2 tbsp sunflower oil
1 onion, finely sliced
1 large carrot, peeled and finely sliced
200g/7oz bacon lardons
50g/2oz plain (all-purpose) flour
150ml/¼ pint /⅔ cup dry white wine
450ml/¾ pint/scant 2 cups chicken stock
2 rabbits, jointed
90g/3½oz chopped, dried apricots
30ml/2 tbsp chopped fresh rosemary
15ml/1 tbsp chopped fresh parsley
salt and ground black pepper

Energy 389kcal/1612kJ; Protein 33g; Carbohydrate 13g, of which sugars 7g; Fat 23g, of which saturates 9g; Cholesterol 99mg; Calcium 64mg; Fibre 3.1g; Sodium 648mg.

SERVES 4–6

8 thin slices prosciutto
30ml/2 tbsp blackberry jelly
15ml/1 tbsp wholegrain mustard
15ml/1 tbsp chopped fresh sage
1 strip loin from a fallow deer,
    cut into 2 to measure about
    20cm/8in long
olive oil for drizzling
100ml/3½ fl oz/scant ½ cup port
200ml/7fl oz/scant 1 cup beef stock
30ml/2 tbsp crème fraîche
salt and ground black pepper
wilted greens, to serve

Energy 201kcal/850kJ; Protein 32g; Carbohydrate
5g, of which sugars 4g; Fat 7g, of which saturates
3g; Cholesterol 78mg; Calcium 23mg; Fibre 0.0g;
Sodium 388mg.

ROAST VENISON WITH PROSCIUTTO

A wood-fired oven at a high temperature is perfect for venison loin; much like a fillet of beef, it needs to cook really quickly to stay moist. This special occasion dish is a wonderful feast for all the senses, served with some sautéed wild mushrooms or wilted spinach and perhaps some buttery polenta. Ask your butcher for a strip loin from a fallow deer, with a diameter of about 7.5cm/3in.

1 Build up the fire in the oven until the temperature reaches 250°C/480°F, this will take about 60 minutes. When it is up to temperature, push the fire to the back of the oven with a metal peel or coal hook. Close the door to keep the heat inside.

2 Layer four of the prosciutto slices so they overlap on a flat surface and do the same with the other slices.

3 In a small bowl, mix together the blackberry jelly, mustard and sage and season well. Spread this mixture over the prosciutto slices.

4 Put each of the pieces of the loin on one of the prosciutto layers and roll up tightly to make a parcel. Place both the parcels in a roasting pan and drizzle over a little olive oil. Place the roasting pan on the oven floor, close to the fire. Leave the door open.

5 Roast the venison for 10–15 minutes, depending on how rare or well-done you like your meat.

6 Take the roasting pan out of the oven and put it on a heatproof surface. Take the meat out of the roasting pan and put it on a plate to rest, covered with foil.

7 Put the roasting pan on the stove over a medium heat and add the port and the beef stock. Stir all the time with a wooden spoon to get any juices off the base of the pan and bring to the boil. Stir in the crème fraîche and bubble for 3–4 minutes. Check the seasoning to see if it needs salt and pepper.

8 Cut the venison into thick slices, and pour any juices that have come out while resting into the gravy. Serve the venison on top of the wilted greens and gravy.

VEGETARIAN AND VEGETABLE SIDE DISHES

Vegetables cooked in the wood-fired oven are a revelation – sweet, intense and earthy. They are delicious as a main course and perfect to accompany many of the recipes in the fish and meat chapters. Use their bright colours and different textures to give variety to your meals and use whatever is in season for stunning results.

FRITTATA VERDE

A frittata is a marvellous thing – a few golden-yolked eggs beaten and then cooked with some simple ingredients. Use whatever herbs you have available – parsley, chives, tarragon or oregano – and experiment to see the different effects. Traditional frittatas are cooked on the hob, but using a wood-fired oven is less likely to dry out the bottom and keeps the insides deliciously moist.

SERVES 4

3 handfuls spinach or chard leaves, washed and finely chopped
4 spring onions (scallions), roughly chopped
15ml/1 tbsp sunflower oil
6 free-range (farm-fresh) eggs
30ml/2 tbsp mixed fresh herbs, roughly chopped
90g/3½oz Cheddar or Gruyere cheese, grated
salt and ground black pepper

VARIATION
....

For a more substantial frittata you could add a few potatoes. Cook them first in salted boiling water until tender, slice thinly, then sauté in the oil before adding the spring onion and spinach. Make sure they are absolutely tender before you mix in the eggs.

---

1 Build up the fire in the oven until the temperature reaches 180°C/350°F, this will take about 40 minutes. Push the fire to the back of the oven with a metal peel or coal hook, and keep the door closed to retain the heat inside.

2 Toss the chopped spinach and spring onions in the oil and put in a small, heavy, ovenproof, non-stick frying pan, with a diameter of about 20cm/8in.

3 Put a lid or a cover on the pan and place the pan on the oven floor. Cook for 4–5 minutes, until the vegetables have wilted.

4 Take out the pan, put it on a heatproof surface and take off the lid. Close the oven door to keep the oven up to temperature.

5 In a large bowl, beat the eggs with the fresh herbs and season well with salt and pepper. Turn the wilted vegetables into the bowl and fold together (make sure you wear oven gloves to pick up the pan, as the handle will still be hot).

6 Put the whole mixture back into the pan and sprinkle the cheese over the top. Put the pan back on the oven floor and close the door. Bake in the oven until the eggs have set and the top is golden, this will take about 10–12 minutes.

7 Take the pan out of the oven. Leave it to stand for a 2–3 minutes before using a heatproof spatula to ease the frittata away from the bottom of the pan and turn it on to a plate.

8 Serve cut into wedges with boiled new potatoes and a tomato and shallot salad. The frittata is also delicious served cold as part of a picnic.

Energy 273kcal/1134kJ; Protein 18g; Carbohydrate 2g, of which sugars 1g; Fat 22g, of which saturates 1g; Cholesterol 379mg; Calcium 308mg; Fibre 1.7g; Sodium 443mg.

COURGETTE, MINT AND FETA FRITTERS

These fritters are a great snack, delicious straight out of the wood-fired oven, where they cook very quickly in the intense heat, becoming brown outside and meltingly tender inside. You can substitute finely grated carrot or butternut squash for the courgette, to vary the result. Small fritters make wonderful finger food for a crowd – they look stunning and smell amazing, and will delight your guests.

1 Build up the fire on the base of the oven until the temperature gets to 220°C/425°F. This will take about 60 minutes. Push the fire to the back of the oven with a metal peel or coal hook, and keep the door closed to maintain the temperature.

2 Grate the peeled courgettes on to a board, then squeeze the juices out, using your hands, a handful at a time, and transfer to a large bowl as you go.

3 Beat the eggs in another bowl and whisk in the flour. Fold in the squeezed courgettes, herbs and feta cheese. Season well.

4 Put the oil in a heavy, non-stick, ovenproof frying pan. Place the pan on the oven floor to heat the oil. Close the door until the oil heats up, which should take about 1 minute.

5 When the oil is hot, put about six spoonfuls of the mixture around the pan. Put the pan back in the oven and close the door.

6 Cook the fritters for 5 minutes, until golden, then turn and cook the other side. Take the pan out of the oven and remove the fritters from the pan. Continue cooking in batches until all the mixture is used up. Serve warm with a little fresh herb and rocket salad.

SERVES 6 AS AN APPETIZER

4 medium courgettes (zucchini), peeled
2 eggs
50g/2oz plain (all-purpose) flour
30ml/2 tbsp freshly chopped mint
30ml/2 tbsp chopped fresh chives
90g/3oz feta cheese, crumbled into small pieces
sunflower oil, for frying
salt and ground black pepper
herb and rocket (arugula) salad, to serve

Energy 207kcal/859kJ; Protein 7g; Carbohydrate 10g, of which sugars 2g; Fat 16g, of which saturates 4g; Cholesterol 88mg; Calcium 104mg; Fibre 0.4g; Sodium 311mg.

25g/1oz dried wild mushrooms
1 medium leek, washed and
   finely sliced
115g/4oz button (white)
   mushrooms, sliced
1 clove garlic, peeled and crushed
30ml/2 tbsp olive oil
25g/1oz butter
300g/11oz Arborio rice
150ml/¼ pint/⅔ cup dry white wine
hot vegetable stock
30ml/2 tbsp crème fraîche
115g/4oz Parmesan cheese, grated
45ml/3 tbsp chopped fresh chives
salt and ground black pepper
green salad, to serve

Energy 380kcal/1559kJ; Protein12g; Carbohydrate
10g, of which sugars 2g; Fat 16g, of which saturates
4g; Cholesterol 35mg; Calcium 221mg; Fibre 3.4g;
Sodium 284mg.

OVEN-BAKED MUSHROOM RISOTTO

Risotto is perfect for any time of year – it can be light and fragrant in the spring and summer or earthy and heart-warming for the autumn and winter. Traditionally, risotto is made by stirring constantly on the stove, however slow-cooking it in the wood-fired oven works equally well, and is a good way of using a falling oven.

1 Build the fire in the oven so it reaches 180°C/350°F, this will take about 30 minutes. When it is at temperature, push the fire to the back with a metal peel or coal hook.

2 Soak the dried mushrooms in 120ml/ 4fl oz/½ cup boiling water for 30 minutes. Drain, retaining the soaking liquor, and roughly chop the mushrooms.

3 Toss the sliced leek, button mushrooms and garlic with the oil. Put into an ovenproof pan with the butter, cover with a lid and sweat in the oven with the door closed for about 10 minutes, until the leeks have softened.

4 Take the ovenproof dish out of the oven, remove the lid and stir in the Arborio rice along with the soaked wild mushrooms and their soaking liquor.

5 Add the white wine to the pan with just enough hot vegetable stock to cover the rice by 2.5cm/1in. Season with plenty of salt and black pepper.

6 Cover the pan and put back in the oven with the door closed for about 30 minutes, until the rice has absorbed the liquids and is tender. From time to time, take the pan out of the oven and stir the risotto. If the rice has absorbed all the liquid and is still al dente, add a little more hot vegetable stock and return to the oven with the lid on and the door closed.

7 When the rice is tender, stir the crème fraîche, Parmesan and chives into the risotto. Adjust the seasoning with a little more salt and black pepper if necessary and serve immediately with a fresh green salad.

1 medium aubergine (eggplant)
1 red (bell) pepper
1 yellow (bell) pepper
2 medium courgettes (zucchini)
1 red onion, sliced
2 cloves garlic, peeled and sliced
120ml/4fl oz/½ cup olive oil
15ml/1 tbsp harissa paste
45ml/3 tbsp red wine vinegar
30ml/2 tbsp chopped fresh parsley
30ml/2 tbsp chopped fresh mint
90g/3½oz sunflower seeds, toasted
salt and ground black pepper
couscous, to serve

VARIATION

These roasted vegetables are also delicious served at room temperature as a salad to accompany cheeses or cold roasted meats, or in a ciabatta sandwich with goat's cheese.

Energy 312kcal/1292kJ; Protein 5g; Carbohydrate 10g, of which sugars 6g; Fat 28g, of which saturates 4g; Cholesterol 0mg; Calcium 48mg; Fibre 2.3g; Sodium 109mg.

ROAST SUMMER VEGETABLES WITH HARISSA DRESSING

This is the perfect recipe to cook when you have a glut of summer vegetables, as the wood-fired oven brings out their intense natural sweetness. Harissa is a full-flavoured and hugely versatile spice paste from North Africa, which you can use in dips, dressings and stews, and on pizzas and sandwiches.

1 Build up the fire in the oven until the temperature reaches 220°C/425°F. This will take about 60 minutes. Push the fire to the back of the oven with a metal peel or coal hook. Keep the door closed to maintain the oven temperature.

2 Chop the vegetables into roughly equal pieces, about 2.5cm/1in squares, and toss with the onion, garlic and half the oil. Season well with salt and pepper. Transfer to two roasting pans, so they are in a single layer.

3 Carefully place the roasting pans on the oven floor. Close the door.

4 Bake the vegetables in the oven for about 30 minutes, until cooked through, and starting to char at the edges.

5 In a large bowl, mix the harissa paste with the red wine vinegar, the rest of the oil and the parsley and mint. Take the roasting pans out of the oven.

6 Transfer the vegetables to the bowl containing the harissa dressing. Toss the dressing gently through the cooked vegetables and transfer them to a serving dish. Sprinkle over the sunflower seeds. Serve hot or at room temperature with couscous.

STUFFED RED PEPPERS WITH PINE NUTS

The red peppers in this recipe become a more vibrant colour in the wood-fired oven, and the high heat intensifies their natural sweetness while giving them a delicious charring around the edges. This is a great lunch dish with some good fresh bread and a green salad, and it makes a colourful addition to a pizza party.

1 Build up the fire in the oven until the temperature reaches 200°C/400°F, this will take about 50 minutes. Push the fire to the back of the oven with a metal peel or coal hook. Close the door.

2 Put the pine nuts in a small ovenproof frying pan with no oil. Place the frying pan on the oven floor and toast the pine nuts for about 3–4 minutes until golden. Watch them closely, as they burn quickly. Take the pine nuts out of the pan and set aside.

3 Cut the peppers into halves following the natural lines from the top down to the bottom. Don't chop the top of the peppers off before you cut them in half – the rounded ends are needed, to keep the filling in.

4 Cut out any big bits of white pith from the pepper halves. Put the pepper halves into a flat, wide, ovenproof dish.

5 In a bowl, toss the chopped onion with the oregano, cherry tomatoes, orange rind and juice, capers, pine nuts and olive oil. Season well with salt and pepper. Pile the tomato mixture into the pepper halves.

6 Carefully place the dish on the oven floor. Close the door and bake in the oven for 20–30 minutes, until the peppers are tender and slightly charred but still hold their shape.

7 Take the dish out of the oven. Arrange the peppers on a plate and serve hot or at room temperature with some good bread.

SERVES 4

30ml/2 tbsp pine nuts
4 red (bell) peppers
1 red onion, finely chopped
30ml/2 tbsp chopped fresh oregano
115g/4oz cherry tomatoes, cut
   in half
grated rind and juice of 1 orange
15ml/1 tbsp capers, rinsed and
   roughly chopped
45ml/3 tbsp olive oil
salt and ground black pepper

Energy 229kcal/1949kJ; Protein 3g; Carbohydrate 16g, of which sugars 15g; Fat 17g, of which saturates 0g; Cholesterol 99mg; Calcium 29mg; Fibre 2g; Sodium 137mg.

POTATOES PROVENÇAL

This dish is perfect for a sunny early autumn day – when you have an abundance of late summer vegetables and you want to enjoy being outdoors for as long as possible before the return of winter. Make the most of the combination of the tomato and courgette harvests with fragrant fresh herbs and some well-flavoured potatoes, and pop this dish in the wood-fired oven for a couple of hours, perhaps with a shoulder of lamb to slow-roast, and enjoy it later in the evening.

1 Build up the fire in the oven until the temperature reaches 180°C/350°F, this will take about 40 minutes. Push the fire to the back of the oven with a metal peel or coal hook, and close the door.

2 In a large bowl toss together the sliced courgettes, tomatoes, onion, garlic, marjoram and basil with half of the olive oil. Season well with salt and pepper.

3 Slice the potatoes very thinly and place half of them in the base of a large ovenproof dish.

4 Put the courgette mixture on top of the potato layer. Layer the rest of the potatoes on top. Drizzle over the remaining oil and season with salt and pepper.

5 Put the dish on the oven floor. Close the door and cook for 60–90 minutes, until the potatoes are meltingly tender and golden.

6 Take the dish out of the oven, using a metal peel to bring it to the front of the oven. Serve as an accompaniment to roast lamb, or on its own with a green salad.

SERVES 6

2 medium courgettes (zucchini), sliced
4 large ripe tomatoes, sliced
1 red onion, thinly sliced
2 large cloves of garlic, peeled and crushed
30ml/2 tbsp fresh marjoram, roughly chopped
15ml/1 tbsp fresh basil, chopped
90ml/6 tbsp extra virgin olive oil
1kg/2¼lb floury potatoes, peeled
salt and ground black pepper

> **COOK'S TIP**
> You need a floury-textured potato for this recipe, as they absorb the flavours and the juices from the rest of the ingredients. King Edward, Maris Piper and Marfona all work well.

Energy 296kcal/1232kJ; Protein 5g; Carbohydrate 35g, of which sugars 6g; Fat 16g, of which saturates 2g; Cholesterol 0mg; Calcium 52mg; Fibre 4.3g; Sodium 88mg.

SERVES 6

3 large fennel bulbs
2 medium leeks, washed and finely
   sliced
60ml/2fl oz dry white wine
175ml/6fl oz/¾ cup crème fraîche
15ml/1 tbsp fresh thyme leaves
25g/1oz dried white breadcrumbs
25g/1oz freshly grated Parmesan
   cheese
25g/1oz butter
salt and ground black pepper

Energy 208kcal/862kJ; Protein 5g; Carbohydrate 7g,
of which sugars 3g; Fat 18g, of which saturates 12g;
Cholesterol 49mg; Calcium 107mg; Fibre 1.2g;
Sodium 275mg.

BRAISED FENNEL WITH WHITE WINE

When used raw in salads, fennel is fresh, crunchy and similar to aniseed; when cooked it becomes much more tender and mellow. Cooking it as a gratin in the wood-fired oven gives a great result, as the vegetables are creamy and succulent, while the breadcrumb topping is golden brown and crunchy. Put this dish in the wood-fired oven to accompany a roast chicken.

1 Build up the fire in the oven until the temperature reaches 200°C/400°F. This will take about 50 minutes. Push the fire to the back with a metal peel or coal hook, and close the door to maintain the heat.

2 Cut each of the fennel bulbs, from top to bottom, into 6–8 wedges. Shave off and discard most of the core of the wedges but leave a little so they hold together.

3 Put the sliced leeks in the base of an ovenproof dish and cover with the fennel wedges. Add the wine and cover tightly.

4 Place the dish on the oven floor for 20–30 minutes, until the fennel is tender. Take the dish out of the oven and put it on a heatproof surface, then close the oven door to keep the heat inside.

5 In a mixing bowl, combine the crème fraîche with the thyme leaves, breadcrumbs and grated Parmesan. Season well with salt and pepper. Spoon this mixture over the fennel and leeks. Dot the butter over the top of everything.

6 Put the ovenproof dish, without the lid, on the oven floor. Close the door and bake the dish in the oven for 20–30 minutes, until golden brown and crunchy on the top and bubbling hot.

7 Bring the dish to the oven door, using a metal peel to do so, if necessary. Take out the dish and put it on a heatproof surface.

8 Serve the fennel on its own, as an accompaniment to roast chicken, or with cooked brown rice and baked fish.

450g/1lb dried white beans; haricot (navy), butter (lima) or cannellini
1 bulb garlic
3 sprigs fresh sage leaves
2 stalks celery, roughly chopped
100ml/3½fl oz/scant ½ cup dry white wine
100ml/3½fl oz/scant ½ cup olive oil
salt and ground black pepper

Energy 373kcal/1564kJ; Protein 17g; Carbohydrate 39g, of which sugars 2g; Fat 18g, of which saturates 3g; Cholesterol 0mg; Calcium 142mg; Fibre 17.3g; Sodium 104mg.

COOK'S TIP

Serve the beans as a main course with some roasted pumpkin or green vegetables. They are also good as a side dish particularly with the porchetta recipe or a juicy steak. Any leftovers can be made into a fantastic soup with some peppery olive oil drizzled over the top.

WHITE BEANS WITH SAGE AND GARLIC

This is a simple, easy dish to put in the oven after you have baked something at a high temperature, so you can put the dropping temperatures to good use – you can even leave it overnight and reheat it the next day. Dried beans are a great store-cupboard stand-by. Just remember to soak them overnight before you use them, and don't add salt before they are cooked, otherwise they will never soften. Always boil them vigorously for 10 minutes on the hob, to help them tenderize, before slowly cooking them until soft in the wood-fired oven.

1 Soak the beans overnight in a large bowl in plenty of cold water.

2 To cook the beans the next day, the temperature of the wood-fired oven should be around 150°C/300°F. This is reached by either letting the oven cool after baking something at a high temperature, such as bread, and then utilizing the falling oven, or by building the fire until the temperature reaches 150°C/300°F. The latter should take about 30 minutes. Push the fire to the back of the oven with a metal peel or coal hook, and close the door to keep the heat in.

3 Drain the soaked beans and rinse well under cold running water. Transfer them to an ovenproof dish with a lid that fits tightly.

4 Add the whole garlic bulb, sage leaves, celery, wine and olive oil to the beans and cover with cold water up to about 2.5cm/1in over the top of the beans. Do not add any salt, it will prevent the beans from softening.

5 On the stove, bring the pan to the boil and boil vigorously for 10 minutes, to soften the skin. Put the lid on the ovenproof dish and make sure it fits tightly. Add a layer of foil if the lid is loose. Put the covered dish on the oven floor.

6 Close the door and leave to bake until the beans are tender. This will take 1–3 hours, depending on the age of the dried beans. Just keep checking them for tenderness – they should be meltingly soft and creamy. If they are absorbing all the water, which they might if they are cooking for a long time, just add some more boiling water and stir it into the beans.

7 Once the beans are completely soft and tender, take the ovenproof dish out of the oven.

8 Season the beans well with salt and pepper, stir everything gently together and serve, perhaps with slow-roast shoulder of pork, which you could put into the oven to roast at the same time as the beans.

SERVES 6–8

1 large red cabbage, cored and
    finely sliced
2 medium pears, peeled, cored and
    roughly chopped
1 red onion, sliced
50g/2oz raisins
50g/2oz brown sugar
50g/2oz butter, cubed
30ml/2 tbsp red wine vinegar
15ml/1 tbsp ground cinnamon
salt and ground black pepper

Energy 143kcal/598kJ; Protein 1g; Carbohydrate
21g, of which sugars 21g; Fat 6g, of which saturates
4g; Cholesterol 16mg; Calcium 64mg; Fibre 2.5g;
Sodium 108mg.

BRAISED RED CABBAGE WITH RED WINE AND PEARS

Red cabbage is a great winter warmer. It can be cooked slowly, as in this recipe, and
then reheated as needed. It is also fabulous in stir-fries and raw in salads and
coleslaw. Traditionally, cabbage is cooked with apples, but pears can also be used.
This recipe is delicious served with sausages, pork chops or roast duck.

1 Make the most of the falling heat from a
recipe cooked at a higher temperature, or
build up the fire in the oven until the
temperature reaches 150°C/300°F, this will
take about 30 minutes. Push the fire to the
back of the oven with a metal peel or coal
hook, and close the door to retain the heat.

2 In a large bowl, toss the red cabbage with
the pears, red onion, raisins, brown sugar,
butter, vinegar and cinnamon. Season well
with salt and pepper and transfer to an
ovenproof dish, seal with the lid and a layer
of foil if necessary to make an airtight seal.

3 Put the sealed dish on the oven floor, close
the door and leave the cabbage to cook until
tender – it will take 2–3 hours for everything
to braise slowly.

4 From time to time, open the oven door,
take the lid off the dish and stir everything
around to mix it all up before putting the lid
back on, putting the dish back in the oven
and closing the door.

5 When the cabbage is ready it will sit in the
oven, keeping warm until you are ready to eat
as an accompaniment to roast duck or pork.

ROAST SQUASH AND SWEET POTATO MASH WITH CHILLI, GARLIC AND THYME

Autumn squashes and sweet potatoes can be very sweet, so using garlic, chilli and thyme cuts through that sweetness to create a more balanced dish. You can use any kind of pumpkin or yellow squash such as butternut. A whole bulb of garlic may sound like a lot, but roasting makes it incredibly mellow.

1 Build up the fire in the oven until the temperature reaches 190°C/375°F. This will take about 40 minutes. Push the fire to the back with a metal peel or coal hook, and close the door to keep the heat inside.

2 Wash the squash or pumpkin and sweet potatoes and prick with a sharp knife or skewer. Put them whole into a roasting pan with the garlic bulb.

3 Put the roasting pan on the oven floor. Close the door and bake the vegetables in the oven for about 60 minutes, until they are all tender. Test with a skewer for tenderness. The garlic may take less time to roast; if so, just take it out earlier.

4 Take the roasting pan out of the oven and put it on a heatproof surface. Let the vegetables cool until you can handle them and then peel the squash and sweet potatoes. Scoop out and discard the seeds from the squash.

5 Put the cooked flesh in a bowl with the chopped chilli and thyme and the crème fraîche. Season well with salt and pepper. Squeeze the garlic flesh out of the garlic cloves, discarding the skins.

6 Use a wooden spoon to mash everything together to get a smooth purée. Serve immediately or keep warm in the oven covered with some foil.

SERVES 6

1 pumpkin or yellow squash, about 600g/1½lb in weight
450g/1lb sweet potatoes
1 bulb garlic
1 fresh red chilli, seeded, deveined and finely chopped
30ml/2 tbsp fresh thyme leaves, roughly chopped
45ml/3 tbsp crème fraîche
salt and ground black pepper

Energy 139kcal/589kJ; Protein 3g; Carbohydrate 26g, of which sugars 9g; Fat 3g, of which saturates 2g; Cholesterol 8mg; Calcium 82mg; Fibre 1.7g; Sodium 102mg.

SLOW-ROASTED TOMATOES WITH HERBS

Tomatoes in season are full of flavour, but out of season they can be bland and flavourless. Cooking them in the wood-fired oven will intensify the flavour of tomatoes at all times of the year, as it brings out their natural sugars. They are delicious served with eggs for breakfast, tossed through pasta, with grilled meats, or on sourdough toasts for a tapas-style snack.

1 Build up the fire in the oven until the temperature reaches 150°C/300°F, which will take about 30 minutes. Push the fire to the back of the oven with a metal peel or coal hook. Close the door to keep the temperature up.

2 Put the onion slices in an ovenproof frying pan or shallow ovenproof dish with the tomato halves on top.

3 Mix the herbs with the oil and season well with salt and pepper.

4 Spoon the herb mixture over the top of the tomatoes. Open the oven door and carefully place the pan on the oven floor.

5 Roast the tomatoes slowly for about 40–50 minutes, until they are crinkly round the edges and cooked right through, with a little charring on top.

6 Take the frying pan out of the oven and serve the slow-roasted tomatoes on sourdough toasts, rubbed with a little garlic and drizzled with olive oil.

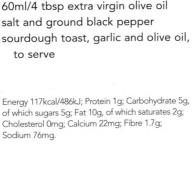

SERVES 6

1 red onion, finely sliced
6 large tomatoes, cut in half
   through the middle
30ml/2 tbsp chopped fresh herbs
   (marjoram, thyme, rosemary,
   chives, fennel or a mixture of all
   of them)
60ml/4 tbsp extra virgin olive oil
salt and ground black pepper
sourdough toast, garlic and olive oil,
   to serve

Energy 117kcal/486kJ; Protein 1g; Carbohydrate 5g, of which sugars 5g; Fat 10g, of which saturates 2g; Cholesterol 0mg; Calcium 22mg; Fibre 1.7g; Sodium 76mg.

1kg/2¼lb shallots, peeled and cut in
  half if large
6 cloves garlic, peeled and left
  whole
3 sprigs fresh rosemary
3 sprigs fresh thyme
15ml/1 tbsp demerara (raw) sugar
90ml/6 tbsp olive oil
30ml/2 tbsp balsamic vinegar
90ml/6 tbsp dry white wine
salt and ground black pepper
cheese and crispbreads, to serve

Energy 199kcal/823kJ; Protein 2g; Carbohydrate
14g, of which sugars 9g; Fat 15g, of which saturates
2g; Cholesterol 0mg; Calcium 45mg; Fibre 2.5g;
Sodium 71mg.

CARAMELIZED ROAST SHALLOTS

This dish can be made in advance and kept in the refrigerator to serve with salads,
cheeses and good breads, and even on pizzas. Baking the shallots in the wood-fired
oven brings out their natural sweetness and also gives them a smokiness that is just
delicious. Serve with most kinds of cheese and some crisp Italian flatbread.

1 Build up the fire in the oven until the
temperature reaches 200°C/400°F. This will
take about 50 minutes. Push the fire to the
back of the oven, and close the door to
maintain the temperature.

2 In a large bowl, toss together the peeled
shallots, garlic cloves, rosemary, thyme,
demerara sugar, olive oil, balsamic vinegar
and wine. Season well. Put everything in a
wide ovenproof dish with a tight-fitting lid.

3 Open the oven door and put the dish on
the oven floor. Close the door and bake the
shallots for about 20 minutes.

4 Open the door and remove the lid from the
dish. If you need to reach in to take the dish
out of the oven, use a metal peel to bring the
dish towards the front of the oven so you can
take the lid off.

5 Close the door and bake the shallots in the
oven, uncovered, for another 30 minutes, until
the liquids have reduced and coated the
shallots with a sticky glaze.

6 Take the dish out of the oven, and transfer
the shallots to a serving dish. Serve hot with a
juicy steak, or leave to cool and serve as an
accompaniment to cold meats and cheeses.

BREADS

Bread has been made in wood-fired ovens for millennia and many people, ourselves included, believe that bread baked like this tastes infinitely better than anything else. The moist air inside the oven helps to develop delicious, chewy crusts whilst the hot oven floor gives a beautiful finish to breads cooked directly on it. Once you've tried baking bread in your wood-fired oven it will be very difficult to settle for store-bought loaves. Fresh yeast is used in most of these recipes; if you prefer to use dried yeast simply use half the amount specified.

WHITE BLOOMER WITH POPPY SEEDS

A bloomer is a traditional type of British bread made from a tight, supportive dough that, for centuries, was cooked on the base of a wood-fired oven. The slashes in the top of the loaf allow it to expand when baking and also look very attractive. The slightly nutty flavour of the poppy seeds adds to the flavour of the bread. This bread is great for sandwiches, try hand cut ham, tomatoes and hot mustard.

1 Build up the fire in the oven until the temperature reaches about 220°C/425°F, this will take about 50 minutes. When the oven is up to temperature, push the fire to the back with a metal peel or a coal hook.

2 In a small bowl, dissolve the yeast in the lukewarm water. Sift the flour and salt into a large bowl, stir in the yeast and water mixture and mix to a soft dough. Turn the dough on to a clean work surface and knead it for about 10 minutes, until smooth, silky and elastic.

3 Place the dough back into the bowl, cover with clear film (plastic wrap) and leave in a warm place to rise for 60 minutes.

4 Turn the dough on to the work surface and shape tightly into a round-ended loaf shape.

5 Cover, and leave it to prove in a warm place for another 30–45 minutes.

6 When the loaf has doubled in size, brush the surface with beaten egg, sprinkle over the poppy seeds and with a sharp knife make diagonal slashes about 2.5cm/1in apart.

7 Sprinkle plenty of flour on to a wooden peel, and transfer the loaf on to it. Place the loaf on the bottom of the oven. Bake with the door closed at about 220°C/425°F for 25–35 minutes, until golden brown, crusty and cooked through.

8 Use oven gloves to turn the loaf over and tap the base of the loaf; if cooked it should sound hollow. Leave to cool completely on a wire rack before slicing.

MAKES 1 MEDIUM LOAF

10g/¼oz fresh yeast
275ml/10fl oz/1 cup lukewarm water
450g/1lb/4 cups strong white bread
   flour
5ml/1 tsp salt
1 egg, beaten
45ml/3 tbsp poppy seeds (or
   sesame seeds, or a mixture)

> **COOK'S TIP**
> ....
> It's very tempting to eat freshly baked bread as soon as it comes out of the oven; however, it is best to leave it for 30 minutes, so that it doesn't cause indigestion. In France commerical bakers are required by law to only sell their loaves after they have been out of the oven for at least 20 minutes.

PER LOAF Energy 1629kcal/6925kJ; Protein 68g; Carbohydrate 339g, of which sugars 6g; Fat 30g, of which saturates 5g; Cholesterol 232mg; Calcium 1237mg; Fibre 17.3g; Sodium 4431mg.

MAKES 2 20CM/8IN BANNOCKS

275/10oz/2½ cups plain
(all-purpose) flour
240g/8½oz/2¼ cups wholemeal
(whole-wheat) flour
150g/5oz rolled oats
5ml/1 tsp salt
15g/½oz bicarbonate of soda
(baking soda)
25g/1oz runny honey
450ml/¾ pint/scant 2 cups
buttermilk or natural (plain)
yogurt

PER LOAF Energy 1354kcal/5748kJ; Protein 53g;
Carbohydrate 262g, of which sugars 33g; Fat 18g,
of which saturates 4g; Cholesterol 25mg; Calcium
727mg; Fibre 20g; Sodium 3252mg.

BANNOCK

A bannock, from the north of England, Scotland or Ireland, is a descendant of the
first kind of bread, which was cooked on a griddle on an open fire. To get a proper
hearth bread finish, bake this directly on the base of the oven so it's good and
crusty on the base and top. Bannock is unyeasted so is quick to make and is
delicious freshly baked for afternoon tea or topped with some smoked salmon.

1 Build the fire in the oven so that it reaches
200°C/400°F. This will take about 40 minutes.
When it is at temperature, push the fire to the
back with a metal peel or coal hook. Close
the door to keep the heat inside.

2 Mix all the dry ingredients in a large bowl.
In another bowl, mix the honey into the
buttermilk or yogurt. Stir this mixture into the
large bowl of dry ingredients and mix
together to get a soft and sticky dough.

3 Turn the dough on to a well-floured surface
and knead briefly until smooth. Cut into two
and shape into two rounds measuring
20cm/8in in diameter.

4 Flatten the tops and cut a large cross in the
top 1cm/½in deep, dividing the bread into
quarters. Use a well-floured wooden peel to
place the bannocks on the oven floor.

5 Close the oven door and leave the
bannocks to bake for 30–40 minutes, until the
base of the loaves sounds hollow when you
tap them. Open the door and use a peel to
bring them toward the door entrance. Take
out the bannocks and cool on a wire rack.

6 After the bannocks have cooled, serve with
butter and smoked salmon. This bread
doesn't keep well, so eat it fresh on the day
you make it, or use it for toast the next day.

SIMPLE WHITE SOURDOUGH LOAF

Sourdough makes fantastic bread with good flavour and texture – it keeps well and makes the best toast. The bread is helped to rise by natural yeasts that feed on a starter of flour and water; the fermentation process can be quite slow, depending on the weather and the ambient temperature, but it is definitely worth the wait. You need to make the starter at least three days before you bake your bread.

MAKES 1 LARGE LOAF
250g/9oz/2¼ cups strong white
  bread flour
5ml/1 tsp salt
500g/1¼lb starter (see below)
warm water

FOR THE STARTER
10g/¼oz dried yeast
450ml/¾ pint/scant 2 cups water
375g/13oz/3¼ cups strong white
  bread flour

MAINTAINING THE STARTER

Ideally, sourdough bread is made with a naturally fermented starter to which no yeast is added. However, that is a complicated process that can take weeks, so we use baker's yeast to kick start the process. Look after your starter and keep feeding it as follows.

Add 450ml/¾ pint/scant 2 cups water and 375g/13oz/3¼ cups of strong white bread flour to the leftover starter and leave to stand for another three days or so before using it in the next loaf. If you don't want to use it immediately you can keep it in the refrigerator. Bring it to room temperature to use when needed.

PER LOAF Energy 1284kcal/5464kJ; Protein 44g; Carbohydrate 282g, of which sugars 5g; Fat 5g, of which saturates 1g; Cholesterol 0mg; Calcium 529mg; Fibre 14.5g; Sodium 3943mg.

1 At least three days before baking, make your starter. Mix the yeast, water and flour together and put in a large bowl, covered with a dish towel, leaving it at room temperature for 3–5 days, until bubbles start to form on the surface and it smells slightly vinegary.

2 During the fermentation process you need to stir the mixture with a wooden spoon 2–3 times per day.

3 When you are ready to bake your loaf, put the flour and the salt in a large bowl. Measure 500g/1¼lb of your starter and add it to the flour, mix together with your hand, or a bread scraper, adding enough warm water, a little at a time, to make a soft dough.

4 Knead on a flat surface until the dough is smooth and elastic. Put in a clean bowl and cover with clear film (plastic wrap). Leave in a warm place to rise until doubled in size – this can take 2–3 hours, depending on the temperature and how vigorous the yeasts are.

5 Turn the dough back on to the surface and knock back (punch down). Rest the dough for 10 minutes, then shape into a round. Put in a well-floured basket to rise. This should take about 1½ hours, but may take longer.

6 Build up the fire in the oven to 230°C/450°F, this will take about 50 minutes. When it is up to temperature, push the fire to the back with a metal peel or coal hook.

7 Turn the dough gently out of the basket on to a well-floured wooden peel. Slash the top of the loaf with a sharp knife, place the dough on the floor of the oven and bake with the door closed for 30–40 minutes.

8 Using the wooden peel, bring the loaf out of the oven and tap the base to make sure it sounds hollow. Cool on a wire rack and wait for 30 minutes before serving.

COOK'S TIP
Sourdough breads are often proved in baskets to help the air circulate and maintain the loaf's shape during the long rising process. A colander lined with a very well floured dish towel, or piece of linen, is a perfectly acceptable homemade version.

CLAY POT LOAF

You can bake any bread dough that you would put in a baking tin in a clean, new flowerpot – the pot will give the dough a distinctive quirky shape but also a good, thick crust. It is essential you season the pots before baking the bread in them, which will help keep them non-stick and should prevent any cracking once in the oven (see Cook's Tip and page 12). You can also use very small plant pots, with a diameter of about 5cm/2in, to make cute miniature rolls for your guests.

1 Put the flours and the salt into a large mixing bowl and crumble the yeast over the top. Stir the honey into the warm water, pour over the flour mixture and mix together with a wooden spoon.

2 Turn the dough on to a clean work surface and knead vigorously for 10 minutes, until smooth, shiny and elastic – it will start off quite sticky but dry out as you knead it. Try not to add any more flour, as this will make the loaf heavy.

3 Put the dough into a clean bowl, cover with clear film (plastic wrap) and leave to rise in a warm place for 1–2 hours until roughly doubled in size.

4 Build the fire in the oven to reach 220°C/425°F. This will take about an hour, so do it while the bread is rising. When it is at temperature, push the fire to the back of the oven with a metal peel or coal hook. Leave the door closed to keep the heat inside.

5 Scatter the seeds on to the work surface and turn the dough on top. Knead the seeds into the dough, cut the dough in half and shape each half into a ball to fit into two seasoned clay plant pots (see Cook's Tip).

6 Cover the plant pots with a clean dish towel, and when the dough has reached the rim, sprinkle with a little more flour and mixed seeds. Make slashes in the top of the dough with a sharp knife, if you wish – this helps the loaf expand and looks attractive.

7 Place the plant pots carefully on the base of the oven. Close the door and let the bread bake for 20–25 minutes. To check if the loaves are done, use gauntlets to take out the pots, tip the loaf out, and tap the bottom – it should sound hollow. If not, leave them in the oven for a few more minutes with the door closed.

8 When the pots are out of the oven, let them stand for 5 minutes before turning out the bread and cooling completely on a wire rack. Slice, or tear the bread, and serve with butter and good cheeses.

MAKES 2 LOAVES BAKED IN 12.5CM/5IN FLOWER POTS

225g/8oz/2 cups strong wholemeal (whole-wheat) bread flour
225g/8oz/2 cups strong white bread flour
5ml/1 tsp salt
10g/¼oz fresh yeast
15ml/1 tbsp runny honey
270ml/9½fl oz/generous 1 cup warm water
50g/2oz mixed seeds (pumpkin, sunflower, sesame and poppy)

> **COOK'S TIP**
>
> To season the flower pots you need to brush some 10cm/4in clay flower pots with sunflower oil on the inside and around the rim. Put in the oven when it is cold and build up the fire until the temperature reaches 200°C/400°F, then let the fire cool down and leave the plant pots in until it is quite cold. Oil and heat the pots twice more and make sure you use the pots only for baking.

PER LOAF Energy 933kcal/3951kJ; Protein 36g; Carbohydrate 167g, of which sugars 10g; Fat 18g, of which saturates 3g; Cholesterol 0mg; Calcium 217mg; Fibre 14.8g; Sodium 998mg.

FOCACCIA

These Italian hearth breads are deliciously infused with olive oil and are perfect to bake in a very hot oven. The bread will have more flavour and a lighter texture if made with a pre-fermented starter or 'biga', so you need to start 3 days in advance.

1 For the biga, dissolve the yeast in the water, then mix with the flour until all the flour is absorbed. Cover and leave in a cool place overnight. Longer fermentation will give a more complex flavour and add a little acidity to the bread. In this case you can refrigerate the biga and leave it for up to 72 hours.

2 Build up the fire until the oven is at an even 230°C/450°F, this will take about 60 minutes. When it is up to temperature, push the fire to the back of the oven with a metal peel or coal hook, and close the door.

3 In a small bowl, mix together the water, malt extract, one third of the olive oil and the yeast. In a separate, large bowl mix the salt with the flour.

4 Add the biga to the bowl of flour, then add the water, oil and yeast mixture too. Mix together with your hands until you have a soft, sticky dough. Don't panic at the stickiness of the dough at this stage.

5 Rub oil on your hands and on the table, then transfer the dough on to it. Knead until it is smooth and springy. It will be messy to start with, but keep going. Tip the remaining olive oil in to a tray and tip until the base is coated. Place the dough on the tray. Cover with clear film (plastic wrap) and leave for 1 hour in a warm place.

6 Pat the dough out into a rectangle in the oiled tray and fold it over in thirds, giving a little stretch in each direction. Flip the dough over so that the seam faces downward. This helps to create an open texture in the bread, and incorporates more oil. Cover and leave for a further 30–40 minutes, then repeat the patting out, stretching and folding. Do this another three times. By this time, because you are not knocking out the gas by kneading, the dough will have become huge.

7 Cut the dough into three pieces, taking care not to lose too much gas in the process. Dimple the surface with your fingertips to gently flatten and expand the breads, until each measures about 30 x 20cm/12 x 8in. Cover the dough and leave for another 15 minutes.

8 Drizzle with a little more olive oil and sprinkle coarse sea salt over the surface, then make deep impressions with your fingertips. Use a well-floured wooden peel to place the dough on to the floor of the oven. Bake for 12–18 minutes, or until a deep golden brown. Take the loaves out, and leave to cool on a wire rack.

MAKES 3 LARGE LOAVES

FOR THE BIGA
500g/1¼lb/4½ cups strong white bread flour
500ml/17fl oz/generous 2 cups water, at room temperature
10g/¼oz fresh yeast

FOR THE DOUGH
approx 250ml/8fl oz/1 cup cool water
15ml/1 tbsp malt extract
100ml/3½fl oz/scant 2 cups extra virgin olive oil
10g/¼oz fresh yeast
10ml/2 tsp salt
500g/1¼lb/4½ cups strong white bread flour
all the biga

> **VARIATION**
> Other traditional toppings for focaccia before you bake the loaves, are small sprigs of rosemary or snipped sage, pitted olives or a sprinkling of sesame seeds.

PER LOAF Energy 1445kcal/6103kJ; Protein 39g; Carbohydrate 252g, of which sugars 5g; Fat 38g, of which saturates 5g; Cholesterol 0mg; Calcium 469mg; Fibre 12.7g; Sodium 505mg.

CORNBREAD

This hearth bread became popular among settlers in the southern United States because it was so quick to rustle up, and could be cooked on an open fire. Here, baked in an ovenproof frying pan, the wood-fired oven, colours the bread a golden yellow. Cornbread is often eaten with chilli con carne or Boston baked beans, but you can also serve it for breakfast with crispy bacon, butter and maple syrup.

1 Build up the fire in the oven until it reaches 200°C/400°F, this will take about 40 minutes. When it is up to temperature, push the fire to the back of the oven with a metal peel or coal hook. Keep the oven door closed to maintain the temperature.

2 Oil a 23cm ovenproof frying pan or line a round 23cm/9in cake tin (pan) with baking parchment. Sift the flour, cornmeal, cumin, salt and baking powder into a large bowl. Stir in the milk, eggs, butter, chilli and chives.

3 Pour the mixture into the cake tin or frying pan and sprinkle the cheese on top. Put the tin or frying pan on the floor of the oven. Close the door and bake for 20–25 minutes, until golden brown. Take the cornbread out of the oven and test by inserting a skewer, which should come out clean.

4 Put the cake tin or frying pan on a wire rack to cool for a few minutes, then turn out the cornbread. Peel off the baking parchment and serve warm with butter and maple syrup.

MAKES 1 23cm/9in CORNBREAD

300g/11oz/2¾ cups plain (all-purpose) flour
240g/8½oz/1¾ cups fine cornmeal
5ml/1 tsp ground cumin
5ml/1 tsp salt
5m/1 tsp baking powder
450ml/¾ pint/2 cups milk
3 free-range (farm fresh) eggs, beaten
115g/4oz/½ cup melted butter, cooled but still liquid
1 fresh red chilli, seeded and very finely chopped
30ml/2 tbsp snipped fresh chives
90g/3½oz grated Gruyere cheese
butter and maple syrup, to serve

> **COOK'S TIP**
> Any cornbread leftovers can be crumbled and used as a stuffing for a roast chicken.

PER LOAF Energy 3179kcal/13297kJ; Protein 5g; Carbohydrate 404g, of which sugars 5g; Fat 141g, of which saturates 82g; Cholesterol 346mg; Calcium 1388mg; Fibre 21.7g; Sodium 3899mg.

240g/8½oz/2 cups plain (all-
purpose) flour
5ml/1 tsp baking powder
5ml/1 tsp salt
5ml/1 tsp chilli powder
15ml/1 tbsp chopped fresh
rosemary
15ml/1 tbsp chopped fresh parsley
1 small red onion, very finely
chopped
200g/7oz cooked, mashed
potatoes, cooled
2 free-range (farm fresh) eggs,
beaten
115g/4oz mature (sharp) or
Cheddar cheese, diced

PER LOAF Energy 1737kcal/7311kJ; Protein 78g;
Carbohydrate 219g, of which sugars 9g; Fat 68g, of
which saturates 32g; Cholesterol 592mg; Calcium
1423mg; Fibre 13.1g; Sodium 3613mg.

POTATO BREAD

This is another loaf using baking powder as a raising agent, so it is a quick and easy bread for the wood-fired oven. You can also try the recipe with mashed sweet potato, which gives a beautiful golden colour, and hard goat's cheese. The potato keeps the bread moist, while the oven crisps up the golden brown crust, with the cheese melting over the top. Serve with pickled onions for a rustic lunch.

1 Build up the fire in the oven until the temperature reaches 190°C/375°F, this will take about 40 minutes. When it is up to temperature, push the fire to the back of the oven with a metal peel or coal hook. Leave the door closed to keep the heat inside.

2 Sift the flour, baking powder, salt and chilli powder into a large bowl. Stir in the herbs. Mix in the onion, mashed potato, eggs and half the cheese. with your hands, bringing the ingredients together to form a soft dough.

3 Tip the dough on to a lightly floured surface and knead quickly into a smooth round, approximately 20cm/8in in diameter.

4 Scatter the remaining cubes of cheese on to the top of the dough, pushing them into the dough slightly.

5 Using a well-floured wooden peel, put the dough on the oven floor. Close the door and bake in the oven for 20–25 minutes, until the bread is golden and risen and it sounds hollow when you tap it on its base.

6 Using a wooden peel, take the bread out of the oven and put it on a wire rack to cool. This bread is best enjoyed on the day you make it, once it has cooled, although it does make deliciously crunchy croutons for soup the next day.

150ml/¼ pint/⅔ cup milk
10g/¼oz fresh yeast
450g/1lb/4 cups plain (all-purpose)
  flour
5ml/1 tsp salt
30ml/2 tbsp sunflower oil
150ml/¼ pint/⅔ cup natural (plain)
  yogurt
1 free-range (farm fresh) egg
melted butter or ghee, for brushing

Energy 353kcal/1490kJ; Protein 11g; Carbohydrate
61g, of which sugars 4g; Fat 9g, of which saturates
2g; Cholesterol 45mg; Calcium 191mg; Fibre 2.8g;
Sodium 375mg.

NAAN BREAD

These Indian breads are baked in the fiercely hot tandoor oven, almost as soon as the breads are stuck to the side of the oven they are cooked to perfection. The wood-fired oven may not give quite such an intense heat, but still gives an impressively authentic result. Make sure you are well protected with oven gauntlets.

1 Put the milk in a small bowl and stir in the yeast until smooth. Put the flour and salt in a large bowl and mix well, then add the yeast mixture, oil, yogurt and egg. Mix well and knead on a flat surface for 10 minutes to make a soft, elastic dough.

2 Put the dough back into the bowl and cover with a plastic bag. Leave to rise in a warm place until doubled in size, this will take around 60–90 minutes.

3 Build up the fire in the oven until the temperature reaches 350°C/660°F, this will take about 60 minutes. When it is up to temperature, push the fire to the back of the oven with a metal peel or coal hook. Leave the door closed to keep the heat in the oven.

4 Divide the dough into six pieces and roll them out into the traditional naan teardrop shape, about 25cm/10in long and 15cm/6in wide. Rest for 15–20 minutes, then prick with a fork before baking.

5 Open the oven door. Use a well-floured peel to put the naans on the base of the oven and cook for about 3 minutes, until they puff up, and are golden brown in colour and just beginning to scorch in places. Don't shut the oven door, and turn while cooking if needed.

6 Use the wooden peel to take the naans out of the oven. Brush, while still hot, with melted butter or ghee. Wrap the bread in a clean cloth to keep it warm and moist, and serve hot with a curry or balti.

PITTA BREADS

Another ancient hearth bread, pitta comes from the Middle East and Eastern Mediterranean. The baking process comes to a dramatic end as the pitta breads suddenly puff up in the oven. Keep a clean dish towel ready to cover them once they come out of the oven, so that the bread stays soft and moist.

1 Sift the flour and the salt together into a large bowl. Stir the yeast into the water and pour this liquid into the flour. Stir together to make a very soft dough. Knead the dough on a clean surface until smooth and leave it to rise in a clean bowl covered with plastic wrap for at least an hour, until doubled in size.

2 Build up the fire in the oven until it is about 350°C/660°F, this will take about 60 minutes. When it is up to temperature, push the fire to the back of the oven with a metal peel or coal hook, and close the door to retain the heat.

3 Take the dough out of the bowl and cut into 12 equal pieces. Roll each piece into an oval about 12 x 18cm/4½ x 7in. Put on a well-floured work surface, cover and leave for 20 minutes to prove.

4 Use your wooden peel with plenty of flour on it to put the pitta breads on the oven floor. There is no need to close the door, because they bake very quickly and you will want to see them puff up suddenly. They will take 90–120 seconds to cook through.

5 Take the pitta breads out of the oven using the wooden peel and put them in a basket. Be careful not to overcook the breads, as they quickly become crisp. Cover them with a clean dish cloth to prevent the crust from going hard.

6 When you are ready to eat the pitta bread, slit open the pockets and fill with any kind of filling you prefer, such as hummus, and salad, feta cheese, olives and sliced red onion, or shredded cold roasted meats from your oven.

MAKES ABOUT 12 PITTA BREADS

500g/1¼lb/4½ cups strong white
  bread flour
5ml/1 tsp salt
325–350ml/11¼–12¼fl oz/
  1¼–1½ cups warm water
15g/½oz fresh yeast

Energy 143kcal/607kJ; Protein 5g; Carbohydrate 31g, of which sugars 1g; Fat 1g, of which saturates 0g; Cholesterol 0mg; Calcium 59mg; Fibre 1.6g; Sodium 165mg.

ENGLISH MUFFINS

The milk in English muffins makes them wonderfully soft in the middle, perfect for splitting and eating with butter and jam. Cooking them in the wood-fired oven gives a golden brown and crusty outside with a moist inner crumb; another bonus is they cook very quickly. Traditionally, they would be baked on a griddle and served as a tea-time favourite with jams or preserves and clotted cream, or you could toast them and serve them as part of eggs Benedict as a brunch dish.

MAKES 8–10 MUFFINS

450g/1lb/4 cups strong white bread
 flour
5ml/1 tsp salt
50g/2oz butter
270ml/9½fl oz/generous 1 cup milk,
 gently warmed
15ml/1 tbsp dried yeast
fine semolina, for dusting

Energy 216kcal/912kJ; Protein 6g; Carbohydrate 35g, of which sugars 2g; Fat 7g, of which saturates 4g; Cholesterol 17mg; Calcium 96mg; Fibre 1.7g; Sodium 246mg.

1 Put the flour and salt in a large bowl and rub in the butter. Stir in the milk and yeast and mix to form a soft dough. Put the dough on a flat work surface and knead for 10 minutes, until smooth and silky.

2 Put the dough back into a clean bowl, cover with clear film (plastic wrap) and leave to rise in a warm place for 1–2 hours, until roughly doubled in size.

3 Build up the fire in the oven until it is about 190°C/375°F, this will take about 45 minutes. When it is up to temperature, push the fire to the back of the oven with a metal peel or coal hook.

4 When the dough has risen, roll it out with a rolling pin until it is 2.5cm/1in thick. Use a 5cm/2in or 7.5cm/3in cutter to cut out rounds of dough. For a traditional finish, dip the tops and bottoms of the muffins in fine ground semolina. Leave the rounds on the work surface, cover with a dish towel and allow to rise for another 30 minutes or until puffy.

5 Transfer the rounds of dough to a baking sheet, liberally dusted with flour or fine ground semolina. Put in the oven and close the door.

6 Bake the muffins for just 3 minutes, then open the door, bring the baking sheet to the front, and quickly flip the muffins over with a palette knife or metal spatula. Put the baking sheet of muffins back in the oven, close the door, and bake for another 4–5 minutes, until they are golden brown and are risen.

7 Take the muffins out of the oven and cool on a wire rack, covered with a clean dish towel to prevent them from becoming crusty. Serve warm, split in half, with butter and jam for afternoon tea, or toast them for breakfast the next day.

> **VARIATION**
> Freshly-baked muffins are also lovely served toasted for breakfast with ham, a poached egg and a dollop of fresh Hollandaise sauce.

PUDDINGS AND CAKES

When you're cooking with the wood-fired oven, you usually think of the high heat recipes for pizzas, fish and meats but this chapter shows just how versatile the oven can be as you can cook a whole variety of desserts either in the high heat or the lower temperatures of the falling oven. The fruits and cakes stay deliciously juicy and moist whereas pastry comes out fantastically crisp.

50g/2oz butter, softened

50g/2oz light muscovado (brown)
sugar

350g/12oz young pink rhubarb, cut
into 2.5cm/1in chunks

15g/½oz stem ginger, drained and
finely chopped

350g/12oz/3 cups self-raising (self-
rising) flour

350g/12oz/3 cups caster (superfine)
sugar

4 medium free-range (farm-fresh)
eggs

150ml/¼ pint/⅔ cup natural (plain)
yogurt

15g/½ oz ground ginger

yogurt, cream or stem-ginger ice
cream, to serve

VARIATION

Pears, blackberries and apples
are all delicious with cinnamon
while plums and peaches go
well with nutmeg.

PER CAKE Energy 3581kcal/15176kJ; Protein 65g;
Carbohydrate 690g, of which sugars 439g; Fat 81g,
of which saturates 39g; Cholesterol 1080mg;
Calcium 1738mg; Fibre 21.8g; Sodium 1982mg.

UPSIDE-DOWN RHUBARB AND GINGER CAKE

This is a very adaptable recipe, as you can use whatever fruit is in season, including plums, pears, apples or blackberries. Baking the cake upside down in the wood-fired oven keeps the fruit beautifully juicy, and gives the cake a lovely appearance.

1 Build up the fire in the oven until the temperature reaches 190°C/375°F, this will take about 40 minutes. Push the embers to the back of the oven, using a metal peel or coal hook. Keep the oven door closed to keep the heat inside.

2 Meanwhile butter a 25cm/10in loose-bottomed cake tin (pan), and line the base with baking parchment.

3 In a medium pan, gently melt together the butter and light muscovado sugar. When the butter is melted and combined with the sugar, add the chopped rhubarb and stem ginger to the pan and mix together. Pour the mixture into the base of the cake tin.

4 Put the flour, caster sugar, eggs, yogurt and ground ginger in a large bowl and beat with a wooden spoon until combined. You can do this in a food processor or blender if you wish.

5 Pour the cake mixture over the sugared rhubarb and stem ginger mixture in the cake tin, using a spatula to get it all out. Spread the batter so it is evenly distributed, but don't disturb the layer of fruit. Bang the base of the cake tin on the work surface to dislodge any air bubbles.

6 Put the tin on the oven floor, close the door and bake the cake for 50–60 minutes. Use a wire tray to stand the cake tin on if you wish. If the top of the cake browns too quickly during the cooking time, cover it with a circle of baking parchment. The cake is done when firm to the touch, and an inserted skewer comes out clean.

7 Take the tin out of the oven and put it on a heatproof surface. Let the cake stand in the tin for 5 minutes before turning it on to a wire rack and peeling off the baking parchment.

8 Serve warm as a dessert with some yogurt, cream or stem ginger ice-cream, or cool it completely and cut into wedges to serve with a cup of tea.

APPLE PIE WITH SPICES

Another all-time classic, apple pie is delicious baked in a wood-fired oven, which crisps up the pastry on the top and the bottom of the pie, giving a crunchy outside and a tender fruity inside. Use the lower heat of the oven to cook the eating apples initially and then build up the fire to get a higher temperature for cooking the pastry. This recipe uses a mixture of dessert apples, which hold together well in the pie, and baking apples, which collapse more during cooking; the baking apples provide a contrasting tartness to the sweeter eating apples.

1 Build up the fire in the oven until the temperature reaches 200°C/400°F. When it is up to temperature, which will take about 40 minutes, push the embers to the back of the oven using a metal peel or coal hook. Leave the oven door closed to retain the heat.

2 Put the apple wedges, butter, sugars and spices in an ovenproof dish. Cover the dish tightly with a lid or some foil, and put the dish on the oven floor. Close the door and cook for 12–15 minutes, until the apples are tender, stirring a couple of times during cooking.

3 Take the dish containing the apples out of the oven, and close the door to keep the heat inside.

4 Transfer the apples to a large bowl and gently fold in the lemon juice and rind. Set aside to cool.

5 Line the base of a 25cm/10in deep ovenproof pie dish with one of the sheets of pastry, pressing it into the bases and sides. Spoon the cooled apples in to the pastry-lined pie dish and spread evenly. Lift the second sheet of pastry with the rolling pin and carefully place it on top of the dish.

6 Trim the pastry, using a sharp knife, and crimp the edges together. Make a couple of steam holes in the top of the pie with the knife.

7 Use the trimmings to cut out some pastry leaves or any other pattern to put on top of the pie, if you wish. Stick them to the pie with the beaten egg and brush more of the egg wash all over the top of the pie. Place the pie in the oven for 25–30 minutes, until the pastry is cooked, crisp and golden.

8 Remove the pie from the oven, and rest on a wire rack for 10 minutes. Serve warm with clotted cream, ice cream or custard. Any leftovers can be reheated or eaten cold with a piece of good Cheddar cheese.

VARIATION

If you prefer not to add spices, then add some blackberries in season, some frozen blueberries are great too.

SERVES 6

675g/1½lb eating apples, peeled, cored and cut into wedges
2 large cooking apples, peeled, cored and chopped into 2.5cm/1in pieces
50g/2oz butter
50g/2oz caster (superfine) sugar
50g/2oz light muscovado (brown) sugar
5ml/1 tsp each ground mixed spice, cinnamon and ginger or 15ml/3 tsp apple pie spice
juice and grated rind of 1 lemon
2 pieces ready-rolled shortcrust pastry 30 x 30cm/12 x12in
1 egg, beaten with a pinch of salt
clotted cream, ice cream or custard, to serve

Energy 432kcal/1811kJ; Protein 4g; Carbohydrate 60g, of which sugars 41g; Fat 21g, of which saturates 9g; Cholesterol 66mg; Calcium 64mg; Fibre 4.6g; Sodium 316mg.

PLUM AND BLACKBERRY CRUMBLE

Crumble is another popular dessert, for which you can use practically any seasonal fruit. This is an autumnal version with plums and blackberries. You can have the crumble made up ready to pop in the oven after you have cooked your main course, and it can bake in the falling temperature while you are eating.

1 Build up the fire in the oven until the temperature reaches 190°C/375°F. this will take about 40 minutes. Push the embers to the back of the oven, using a metal peel or coal hook. Close the door to retain the heat.

2 For the topping, pour the flour into a large bowl, and rub the butter in with your fingers until the mixture resembles coarse breadcrumbs. Add the caster sugar and ground cinnamon and mix together.

3 Put the fruit in an ovenproof dish and add the demerara sugar, orange juice and rind, and cornflour. Gently mix everything together.

4 Sprinkle the crumble topping over the fruit. Put the crumble on the floor of the oven and bake for 30 minutes, until the top is golden.

5 Take the crumble out of the oven and place it on a heatproof surface, for a few minutes, before serving with warm custard.

SERVES 6

180g/6¼oz/generous 1½ cup plain (all-purpose) flour
125g/4¼oz butter
50g/2oz caster (superfine) sugar
15ml/1 tbsp ground cinnamon
1kg/2¼lb plums, halved and stoned (pitted)
240g/8½oz blackberries
125g/4¼oz demerara (raw) sugar
juice and grated rind of 1 orange
5ml/1 tsp cornflour (cornstarch)
warm custard, to serve

Energy 406kcal/1709kJ; Protein 4g; Carbohydrate 63g, of which sugars 39g; Fat 17g, of which saturates 10g; Cholesterol 43mg; Calcium 105mg; Fibre 7.6g; Sodium 129mg.

SERVES 6–8

1 rectangular sheet ready-rolled
  puff pastry
90g/3½oz toasted flaked (sliced)
  almonds
3–4 large, very ripe pears, cored
  and quartered
a little beaten egg
60ml/4 tbsp apricot jam
juice of 1 lemon
single (light) cream, to serve

COOK'S TIP

If the pears aren't ripe, poach
the quarters in a little water,
drain and cool before using.

Energy 203kcal/848kJ; Protein 4g; Carbohydrate
23g, of which sugars 16g; Fat 11g, of which
saturates 1g; Cholesterol 10mg; Calcium 52mg;
Fibre 2.0g; Sodium 70mg.

PEAR AND ALMOND OPEN TART

This is a versatile dessert, which works well with plums, apricots and peaches as well
as pears and apples. The puff pastry cooks very well in the wood-fired oven, as the
high heat really makes it rise so that it is light and crispy while charring the edges of
the fruit slightly and keeping it juicy.

1 Build up the fire in the oven until the
temperature reaches 200°C/400°F. This will
take about 50 minutes. When it is up to
temperature, push the embers to the back of
the oven, using a metal peel or coal hook.
Close the oven door to keep the heat inside.

2 Trim the ends of the pastry with a sharp
knife and use floured hands to lift it on to a
greased baking tray, which is lined with
baking parchment. Use the tip of a sharp
knife to mark a 2.5cm/1in margin around the
edge. Prick the base of the pastry with a fork.

3 Melt the apricot jam with the lemon juice in
a small pan on the hob. Simmer for a couple
of minutes.

4 Sprinkle 50g/2oz of the flaked almonds
over the pastry, leaving the margin clear.

5 Slice the pear quarters very thinly and
arrange over the almonds on the pastry, still
leaving the margin clear. Brush two thirds of
the warmed apricot jam over the pear slices.
Brush the margin with the beaten egg.

6 Put the baking sheet on the floor of the
oven. Bake the tart for 20–30 minutes, if the
pastry is browning unevenly, move the baking
sheet around with your metal peel so it
colours evenly on all sides, much like you
would do with a pizza.

7 When the pastry is cooked and golden, and
the pears are cooked through and slightly
charred on top, take the tart out of the oven
and slide on to a wire rack to cool. Reheat the
apricot jam mixture and brush over the pears,
sprinkle over the reserved flaked almonds,
and serve in slices with pouring cream.

MAKES 16 MERINGUES

4 egg whites
225g/8oz caster (superfine) sugar
whipped cream and mixed berries,
  to serve

> **VARIATION**
>
> You can also serve the
> meringues with roast peaches
> with amaretti (page 121).
>   Try making mini meringues,
> which are fantastic for passing
> round at a party, maybe with a
> little lemon curd in the cream
> to give it a bit of zing.

Energy 58kcal/248kJ; Protein 1g; Carbohydrate 15g,
of which sugars 15g; Fat 0g, Cholesterol 0mg;
Calcium 2mg; Fibre 0.0g; Sodium 16mg.

MERINGUES

You need a very low temperature to cook meringues on the outside and keep them slightly gooey on the inside, so leaving them overnight in a cooling oven is perfect. You can put the meringues in the oven at the end of the day, and just let them sit there until the next morning. They store well, too, so are worth making in quantity.

1 The oven needs to have cooled to around 100°C/200°F when you put the meringues in, and then needs to fall in temperature, so don't worry about keeping the fire built up. Line a baking sheet with baking parchment.

2 Whisk the egg whites until completely dry and stiff. You should be able to hold the bowl upside down without any dropping out.

3 Whisk in the caster sugar until the mixture is glossy. Spoon tablespoonfuls of the mixture on to the baking sheets, or pipe them with a piping bag – eight on each baking sheet.

4 Place the baking sheets on the oven floor. Close the door and bake for 2 hours or until they peel off the baking parchment without sticking, or leave the door ajar and leave them in the cooling oven overnight.

5 When the meringues are firm, or the following morning, open the oven door and take out the baking sheets. Peel the baking parchment off the meringues and if still warm leave to stand on a wire tray.

6 Serve, with whipped cream and a selection of fresh berries.

ROAST PEACHES WITH AMARETTI

This is a lovely way of cooking slightly unripe fruit. The wood-fired oven helps concentrate its flavour, as well as making it deliciously tender and developing its natural sweetness. Serve straight out of the oven, topped with toasted almonds and whipped cream, or try them on a piece of buttery brioche with yogurt for breakfast.

1 Build up the fire in the oven until the temperature reaches 200°C/400°F. When it is up to temperature, which will take about 50 minutes, push the embers to the back of the oven, using a metal peel or coal hook. Close the door to keep the heat inside.

2 Halve and stone (pit) the peaches and finely chop one of them. Put the chopped peach in a bowl with the crumbled amaretti, softened butter, demerara sugar and raspberries. Crush these ingredients together.

3 Put the halved peaches in a roasting pan, cut-side up, and spoon the amaretti mixture equally inside the cavities.

4 Place the roasting pan on the oven floor, and bake the peaches for around 30 minutes, until they are tender and starting to caramelize slightly, but still holding their shape (the cooking time will depend on how ripe the peaches were to start with).

5 Take the roasting pan out of the oven and transfer the peach halves to a serving plate, spooning over any juices that have come out during cooking.

6 Cool the cooked peaches slightly before dusting with icing sugar. Sprinkle over the flaked almonds, and serve, topped with some softly whipped cream or crème fraîche.

SERVES 6

7 fresh peaches
3 amaretti biscuits, crumbled (use the double-baked Italian ones wrapped in paper if you can)
25g/1oz butter, softened
25g/1oz demerara (raw) sugar
90g/3½oz raspberries
icing (confectioners') sugar and 30ml/2 tbsp toasted flaked (sliced) almonds, to garnish
whipped cream, to serve

Energy 146kcal/614kJ; Protein 2g; Carbohydrate 20g, of which sugars 18g; Fat 7g, of which saturates 3g; Cholesterol 11mg; Calcium 20mg; Fibre 4.2g; Sodium 60mg.

CHOCOLATE BROWNIES

A good chocolate brownie is irresistible – dark, moist and slightly chewy. Baking brownies in the wood-fired oven works well, and you can put them in at a low temperature, which will let the top set while keeping the base moist. Let the brownies cool in the tin, as it is then easier to cut into pieces; if you can't wait, just spoon them out of the tin while warm and serve with good-quality vanilla ice cream.

1 Build up the fire in the oven until the temperature reaches 150°C/300°F. This will take about 30 minutes. When it is up to temperature, push the fire to the back of the oven with a metal peel or coal hook.

2 Grease and line a 24 x 24cm/9½ x 9½in square tin (pan) with baking parchment.

3 Put the butter and chocolate chips in a heavy ovenproof pan. Put the lid on and place on the oven floor for around 5 minutes, with the door closed, until the butter and chocolate have just melted.

4 Take the pan out of the oven and gently stir the chocolate and butter together – don't be too vigorous, otherwise the chocolate will crystallize. Set aside to cool.

5 In a large bowl, use a balloon whisk to beat the eggs and sugar until thick and creamy.

6 Sift the flour into a bowl and stir in the ground almonds.

7 Pour the butter and chocolate mixture into the beaten egg and sugar mixture and mix until well combined. Gently fold the ground almonds and flour into the chocolate mixture with a metal spoon.

8 Transfer to the lined baking tin and put in the oven on a wire rack. Close the door and bake for about 30 minutes, until slightly risen. Keep checking so that the brownies don't overcook; the sides should be just leaving the tin, the top should be firm but the underneath still very soft and unset.

9 Take the brownies of the oven and cool in the tin. They will continue to firm up as they cool, so don't worry if they seem underdone. When cool, cut into squares and serve, dusted with cocoa powder or icing sugar.

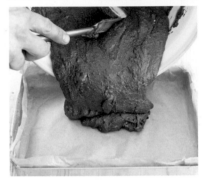

MAKES 16 BROWNIES

125g/4¼oz butter
240g/8½oz dark (bittersweet)
   chocolate chips (no less than
   60–70% cocoa fat)
4 eggs
240g/8½oz caster (superfine) sugar
25g/1oz plain (all-purpose) flour
50g/2oz ground almonds
cocoa powder or icing
   (confectioners') sugar, for dusting

> **VARIATION**
> If you cut the brownies into tiny squares, they are perfect to serve at the end of a supper party, giving a hit of sweetness and dark chocolate without being too filling.

Energy 243kcal/1018kJ; Protein 4g; Carbohydrate 27g, of which sugars 25g; Fat 14g, of which saturates 7g; Cholesterol 75mg; Calcium 28mg; Fibre 0.6g; Sodium 69mg.

MAKES 1 LARGE 25CM/10IN CAKE

275g/10oz/2½ cups caster
   (superfine) sugar
3 large eggs
275g/10oz/2½ cups self-raising (self-
   rising) flour
90g/3½oz flaked (sliced) almonds,
   toasted
120ml/4fl oz/½ cup light, fruity
   olive oil
3 ripe nectarines, stoned (pitted),
   quartered and cut into wedges
125g/4¼oz raspberries
icing (confectioners') sugar, for
   dusting
crème fraîche or Greek (US strained
   plain) yogurt, to serve

Energy 3794kcal/15951kJ; Protein 51g;
Carbohydrate 540g, of which sugars 337g; Fat
174g, of which saturates 22g; Cholesterol 0mg;
Calcium 1250mg; Fibre 40.6g; Sodium 1006mg.

OLIVE OIL CAKE WITH NECTARINES AND RASPBERRIES

Using olive oil instead of butter creates a lighter, moister cake – use a light, fruity olive oil, not a peppery, extra virgin one. Use different fruits such as plums and blueberries or apricots and strawberries if you wish. If you are eating this as a dessert, just put the cake in the oven while you are eating your main course and you can enjoy it hot, with some crème fraîche melting over it.

1 Build up the fire in the oven until the temperature reaches 190°C/375°F. When it is up to temperature, which will take about 40 minutes, push the embers to the back of the oven, using a metal peel or coal hook. Close the oven door to maintain the temperature.

2 Grease a 25cm/10in loose-bottomed round cake tin (pan) with butter, and line with baking parchment.

3 In a large bowl, whisk together the sugar and eggs until thick and creamy.

4 Fold in the flour, flaked almonds, olive oil, nectarine wedges and raspberries and pour the mixture into the prepared tin.

5 Bake for about 40 minutes, until the cake is golden brown on top, firm to the touch, and cooked through.

6 Take the cake out of the oven and leave to stand in the tin for 10 minutes before removing and transferring the cake on to a plate, dust with icing sugar and serve warm with crème fraîche or Greek yogurt.

RICH FRUIT CAKE

This is a great cake to have in your store cupboard. It keeps very well in an airtight container and is delicious with a good cup of tea and a slice of cheese. Just remember, you need to soak the fruit in the tea overnight, so start a day ahead of when you want to bake the cake. Baking the cake in the wood-fired oven works really well because you can utilize the heat produced from cooking something that needs a higher temperature and you won't waste the heat.

MAKES 1 LARGE 25CM/10IN CAKE

350g/12oz raisins
200g/7oz chopped dried apricots
200g/7oz dried cranberries
400ml/14fl oz/1⅔ cups hot tea
225g/8oz butter
240g/8½oz light muscovado
   (brown) sugar
4 free-range (farm-fresh) eggs
250g/9oz/2¼ cups self-raising (self-
   rising) flour
15ml/1 tbsp mixed spice

PER CAKE Energy 5180kcal/21794kJ; Protein 71g; Carbohydrate 759g, of which sugars 580g; Fat 230g, of which saturates 133g; Cholesterol 1463mg; Calcium 1420mg; Fibre 83.9g; Sodium 2915mg.

1 Put the dried fruit in a bowl and stir in the hot tea. Cover and leave to soak overnight.

2 The next day, plan your cake around using the falling oven when the temperature has dropped to about 150°C/300°F.

3 Butter a 25cm/10in round cake tin (pan) and line the base and sides with baking parchment.

4 With a wooden spoon in a large bowl, or in a food processor, beat the butter into the muscovado sugar until light and fluffy, then add the eggs one at a time, beating thoroughly each time.

5 With a metal spoon, gently fold the flour and mixed spice into the butter, sugar and egg mixture, then stir in the soaked dried fruit.

6 Turn the cake mixture into the lined cake tin, smoothing the top and banging the tin on the surface to lose any air bubbles.

7 Put the cake tin on the oven floor. Close the door and bake the cake in the oven for 2½ to 3 hours or until the cake is firm and an inserted skewer comes out clean. If the top browns too quickly during cooking, cover it with a circle of baking parchment cut to fit.

8 Take the cake tin out of the oven. Leave the cake in the tin for 10 minutes on a heatproof surface and then turn the cake on to a wire rack to cool.

9 Wrap in foil and keep until needed in an airtight container, the cake improves if you leave it for a couple of days. Cut into wedges and serve with some excellent tea, and a slice of Wensleydale cheese if you wish.

> **VARIATION**
> We've also made this cake with a mixture of tropical drief fruits such as mangoes, papaya and pineapple, adding a touch of rum in the soaking liquid. You can also make a Christmas version if you wish, using brandy as the soaking liquid.

INDEX

BIBLIOGRAPHY

English Bread and Yeast Cookery by Elizabeth David; *Flavours of Greece* by Rosie Barron; *Building a Wood-fired Oven for Bread and Pizza* by Tom Jaine; *The Wine Roads of Spain* by Marc Millon; *The Art of Dining: A History of Cooking and Eating* by Sara Paston Williams; *Fish: The Complete Fish and Seafood Companion* by Mitch Tonks.

ACKNOWLEDGEMENTS

The authors would like to thank photographer Jake Eastham and food stylist Fergal Connolly for such lovely images. Thanks, too, to all at Anness, especially Joanne Rippin for her outstanding editorial management. Grateful acknowledgement, too, to Jay Emery from Dingley Dell Enterprises (www.dingley-dell.com) for the technical advice on the construction and use of wood-fired ovens.
The Publishers would like to thank Alamy for permission to use their images on pages: 6 (bottom), and 7 (top right and bottom).